For all curious and imaginative children, who find magic and fun in the company of the most adorable felines! Let this coloring book be an exciting journey, where each page is an invitation to explore a world of colors and creativity. May each stroke be an adventure, each color a discovery, filling your days with smiles and special moments alongside these charming felines.

With special thanks to God, whose kindness and inspiration permeate our lives, and also to my wife Regina and my son Guilherme, whose love and support make every step of this journey possible. May this book be a reminder of how blessed we are to have each other.

With all your affection.

Alex Pimentel
2024

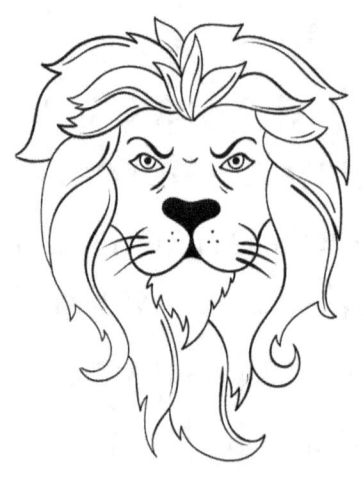
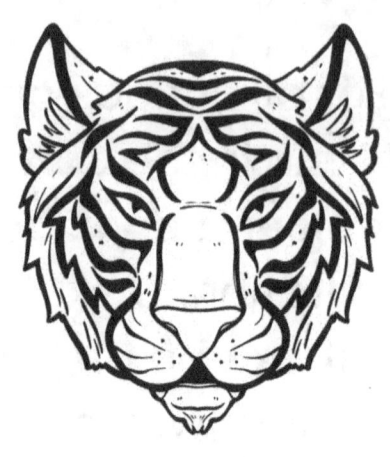

This Book Belongs to:

_____

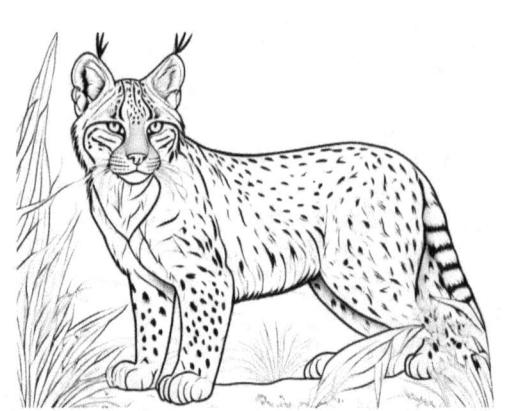
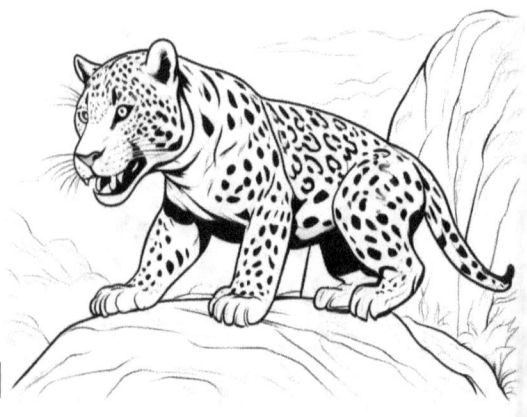

A.P.P®
all right reserved

ALL RIGHTS RESERVED©
2024

No part of this publication may be reproduced, distributed, or transmitted in any form or by any means, including photocopying, recording, or other electronic or mechanical methods, without the prior written permission of the publisher, except for brief quotations incorporated in critical reviews and other specific noncommercial uses. Any unauthorized replica of this work is prohibited.

A.P.P.©

alex's pimentel publications

Test Color Page

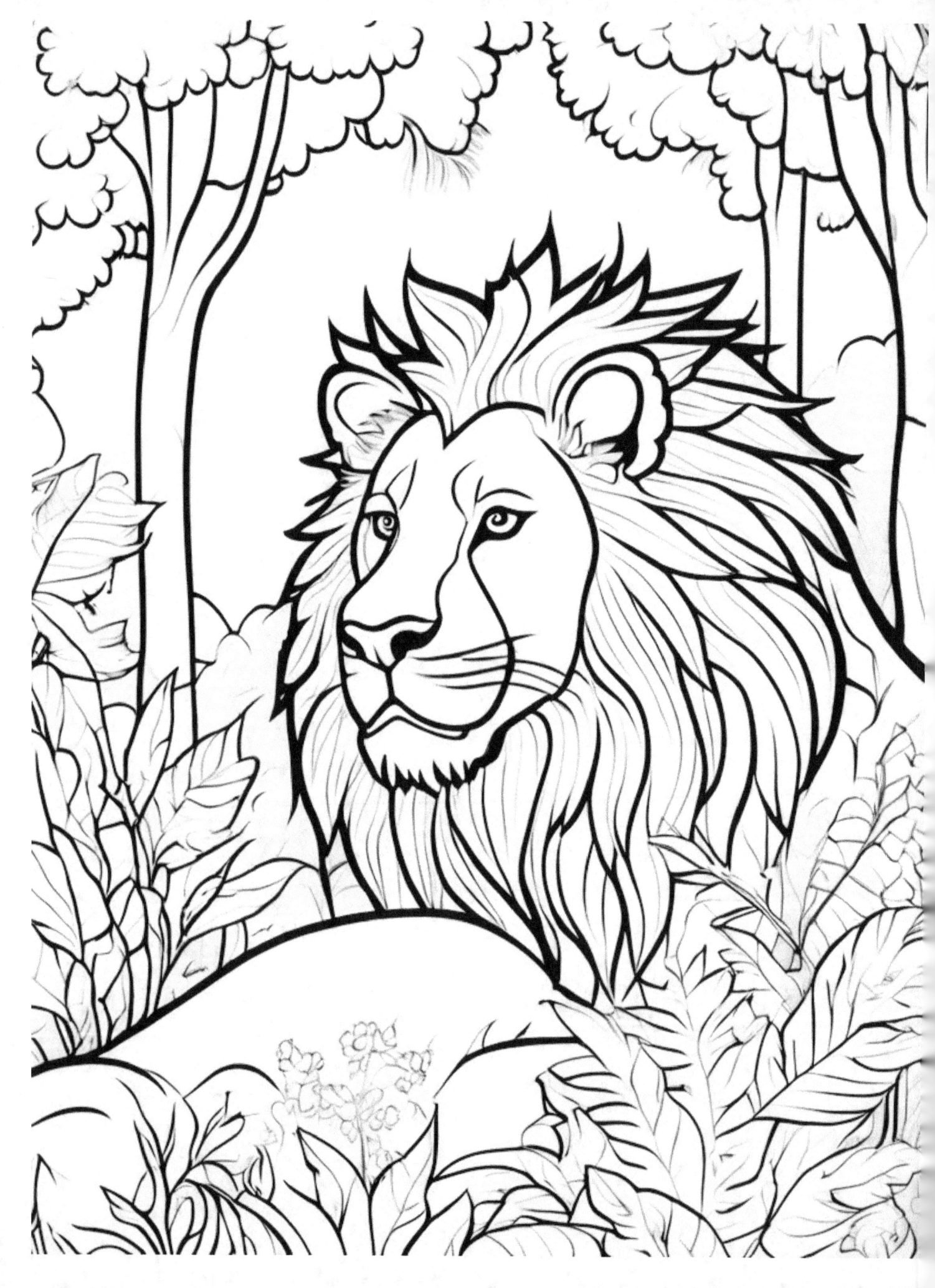

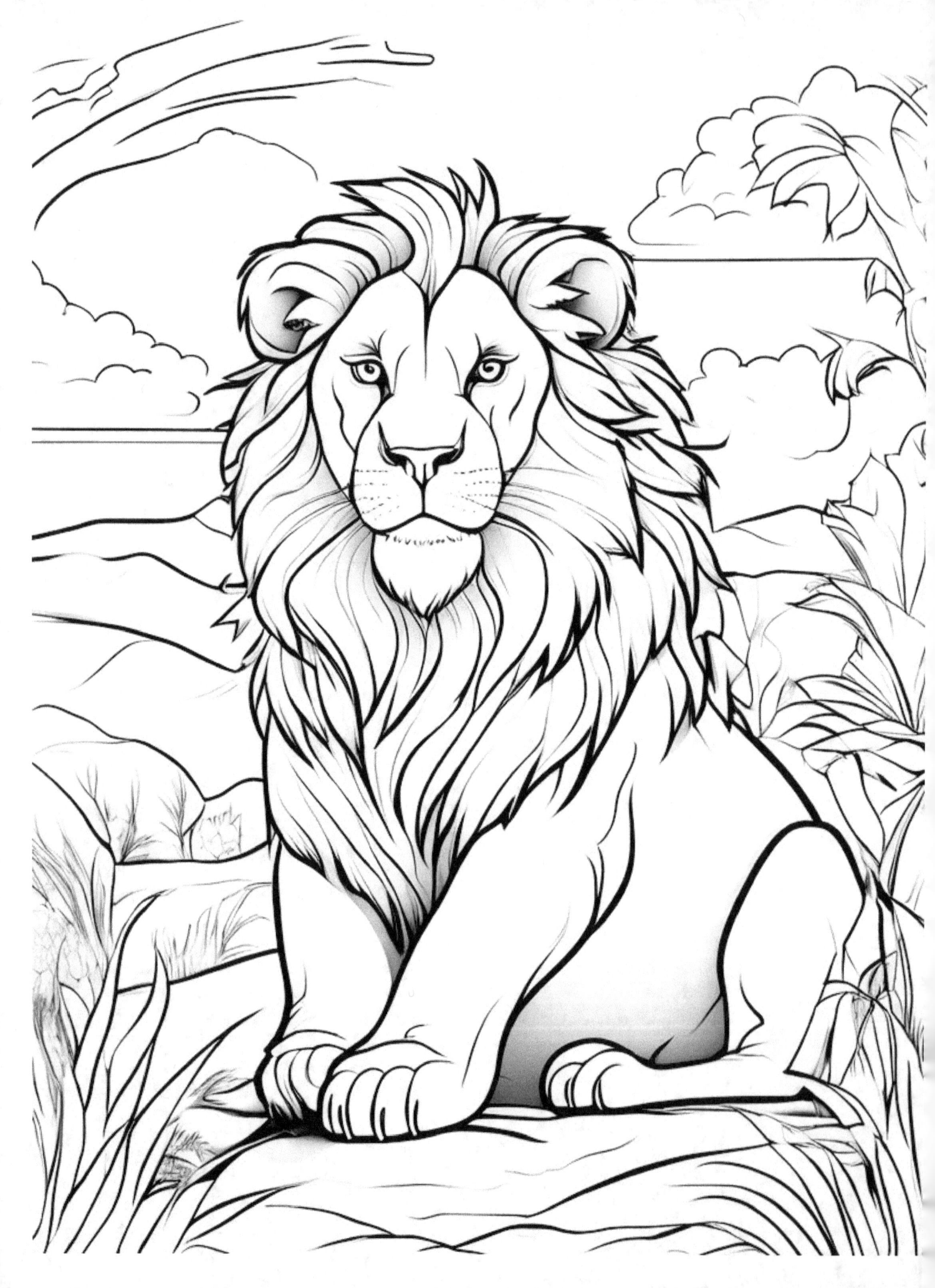

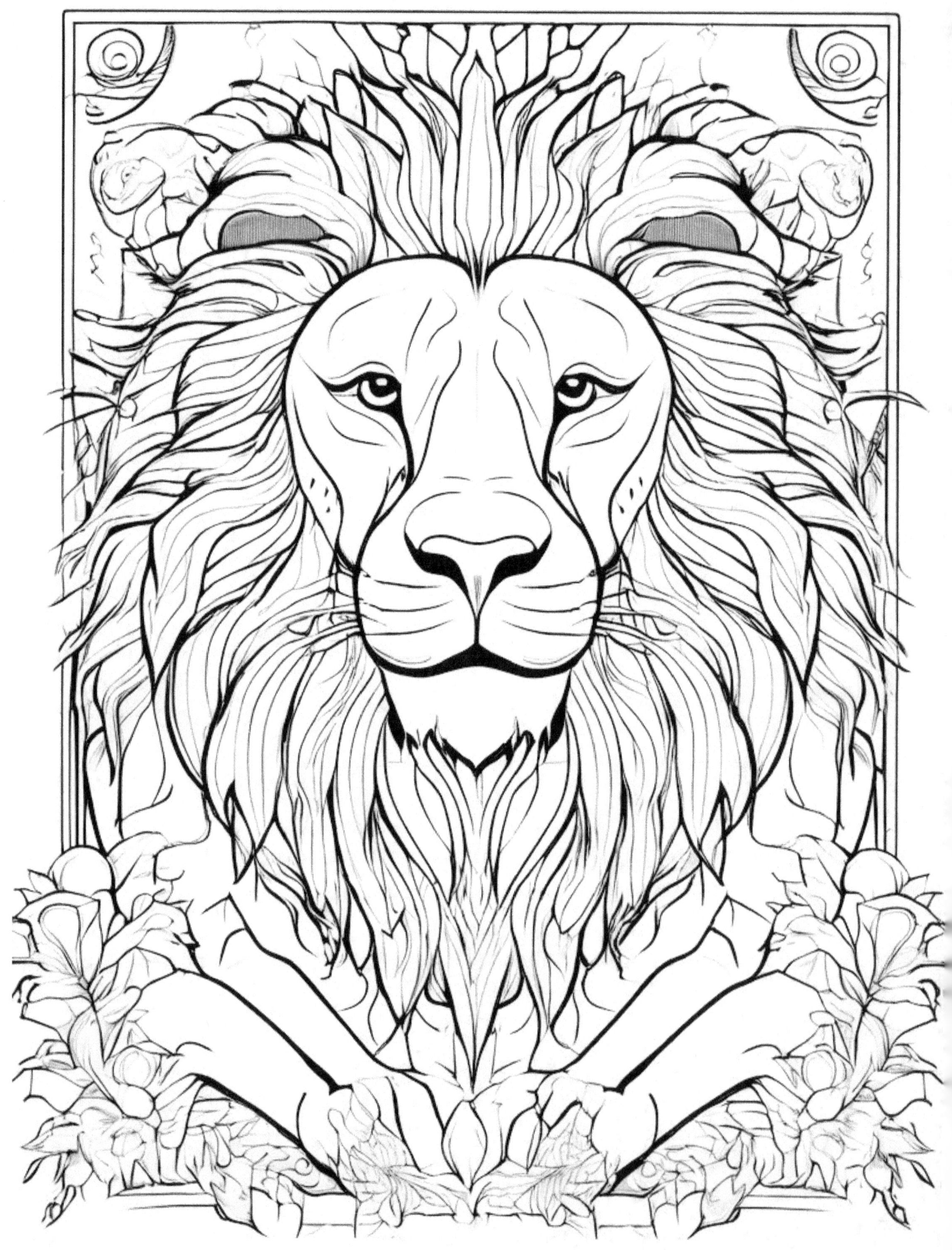

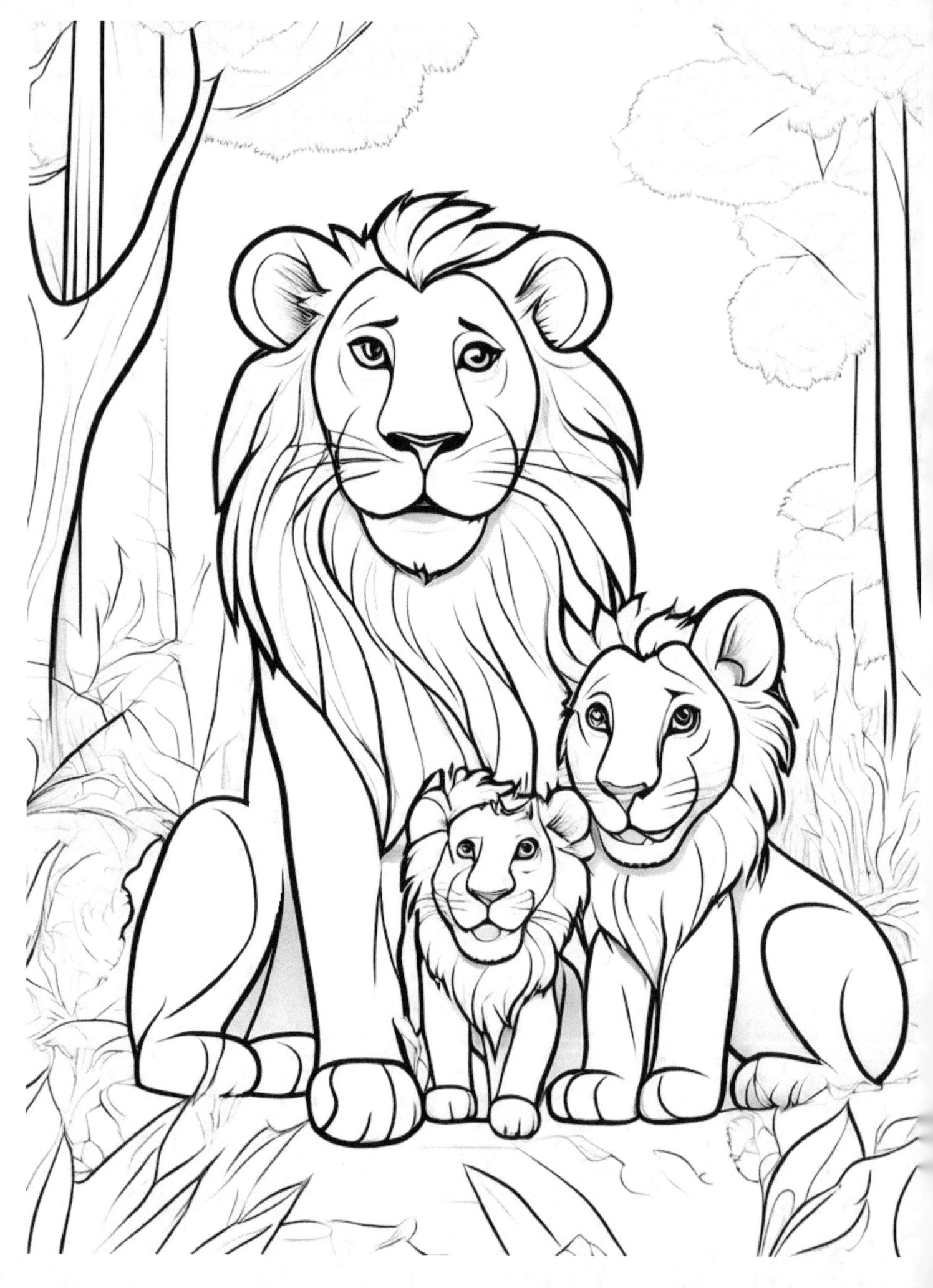

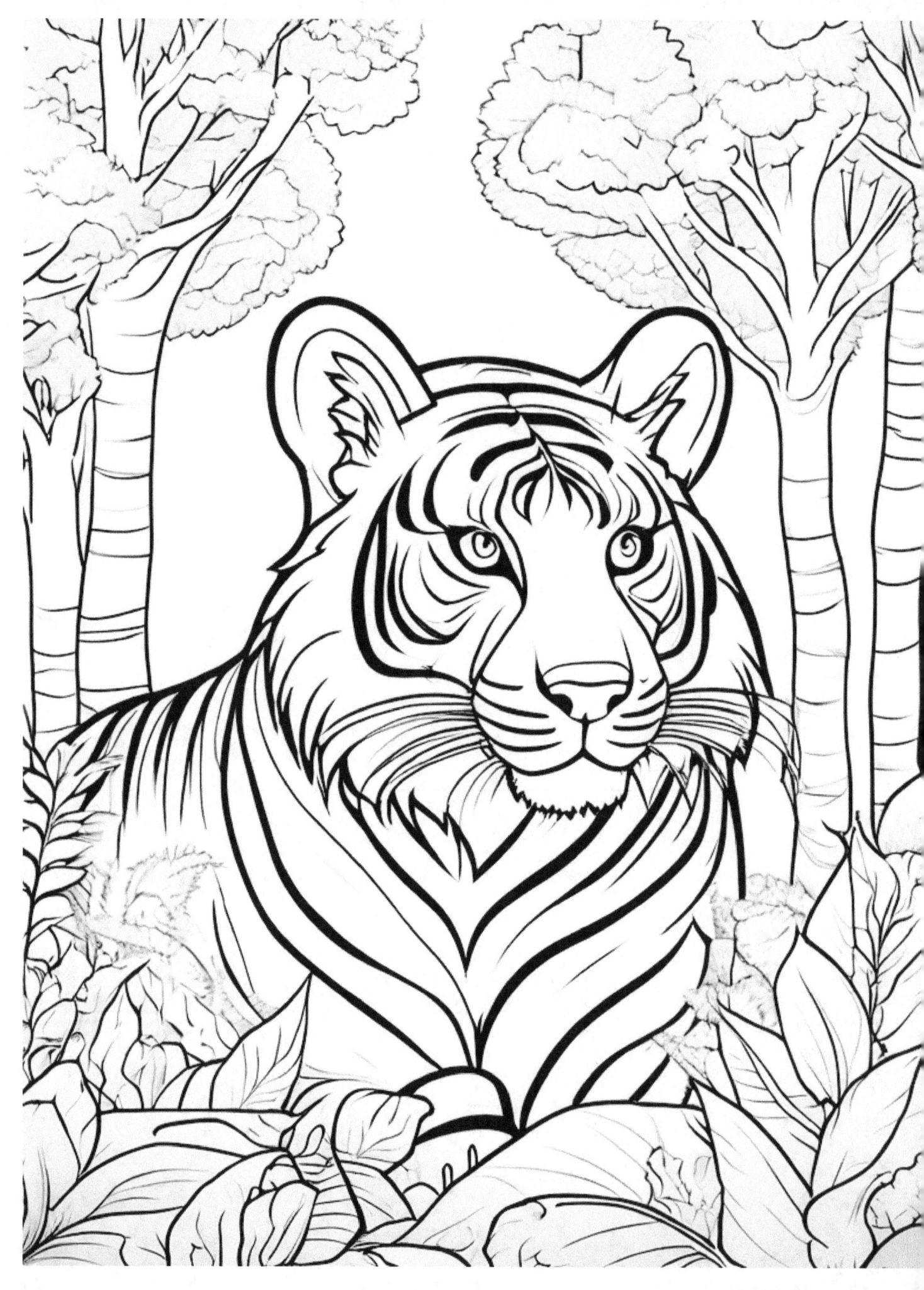

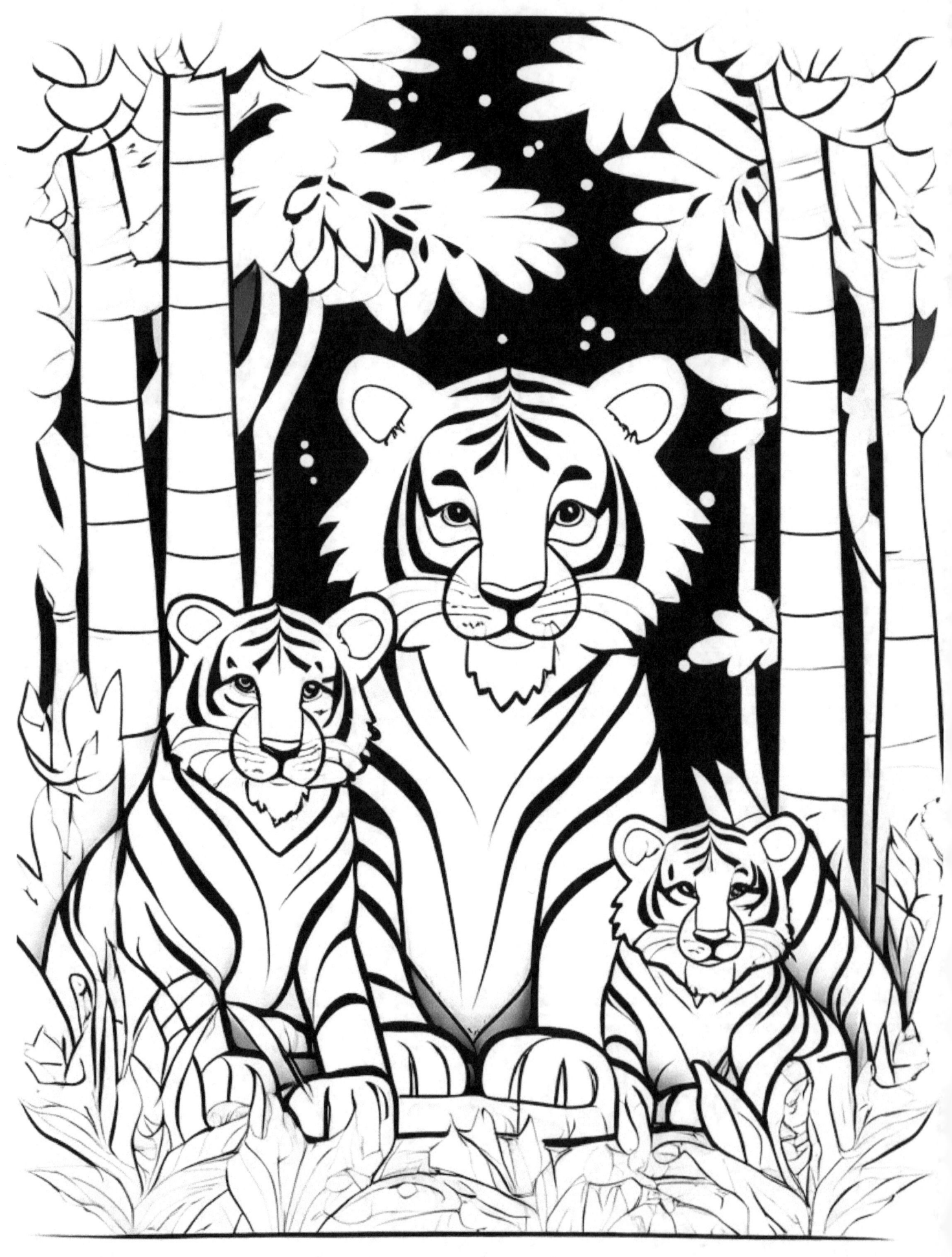

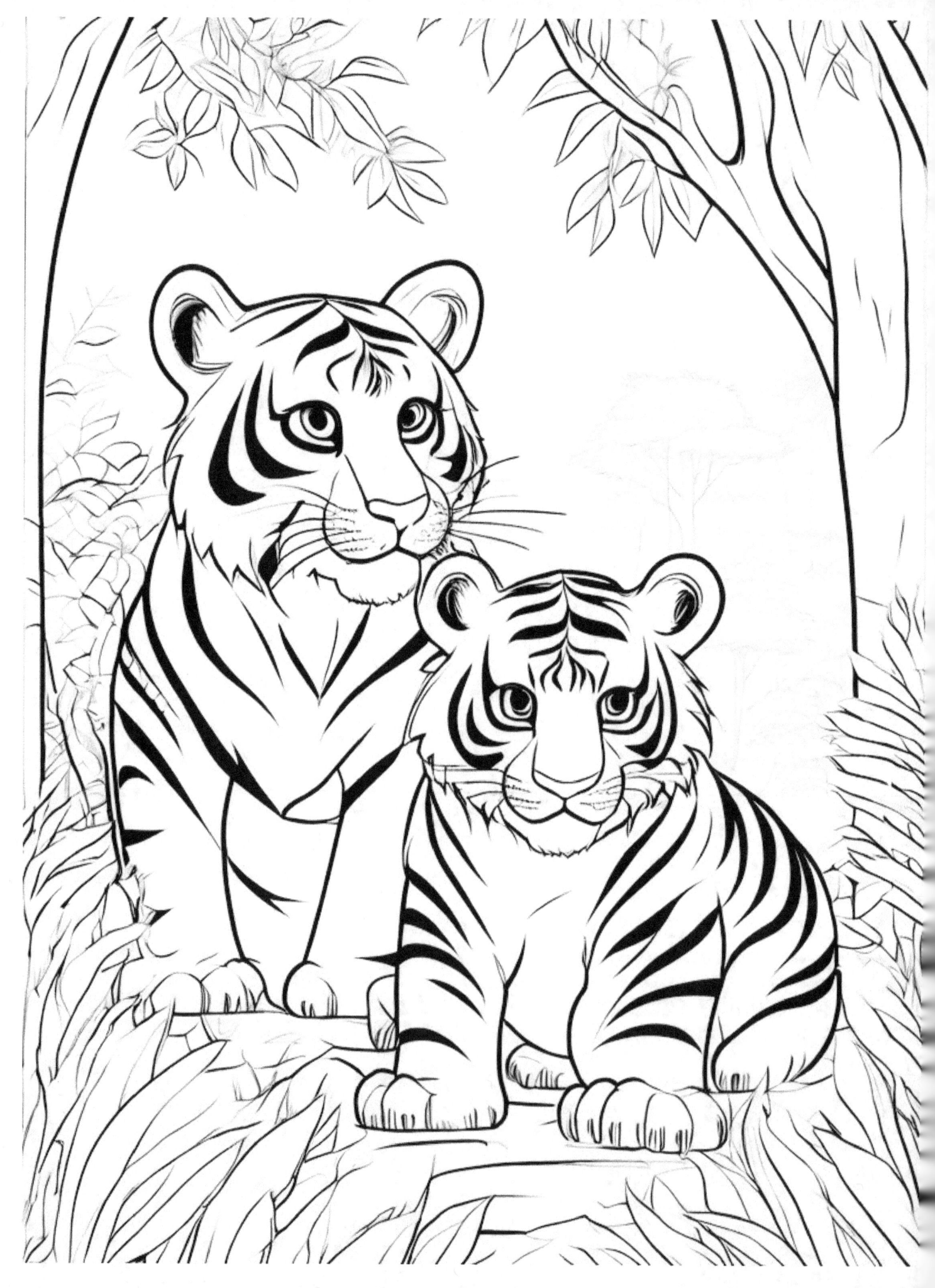

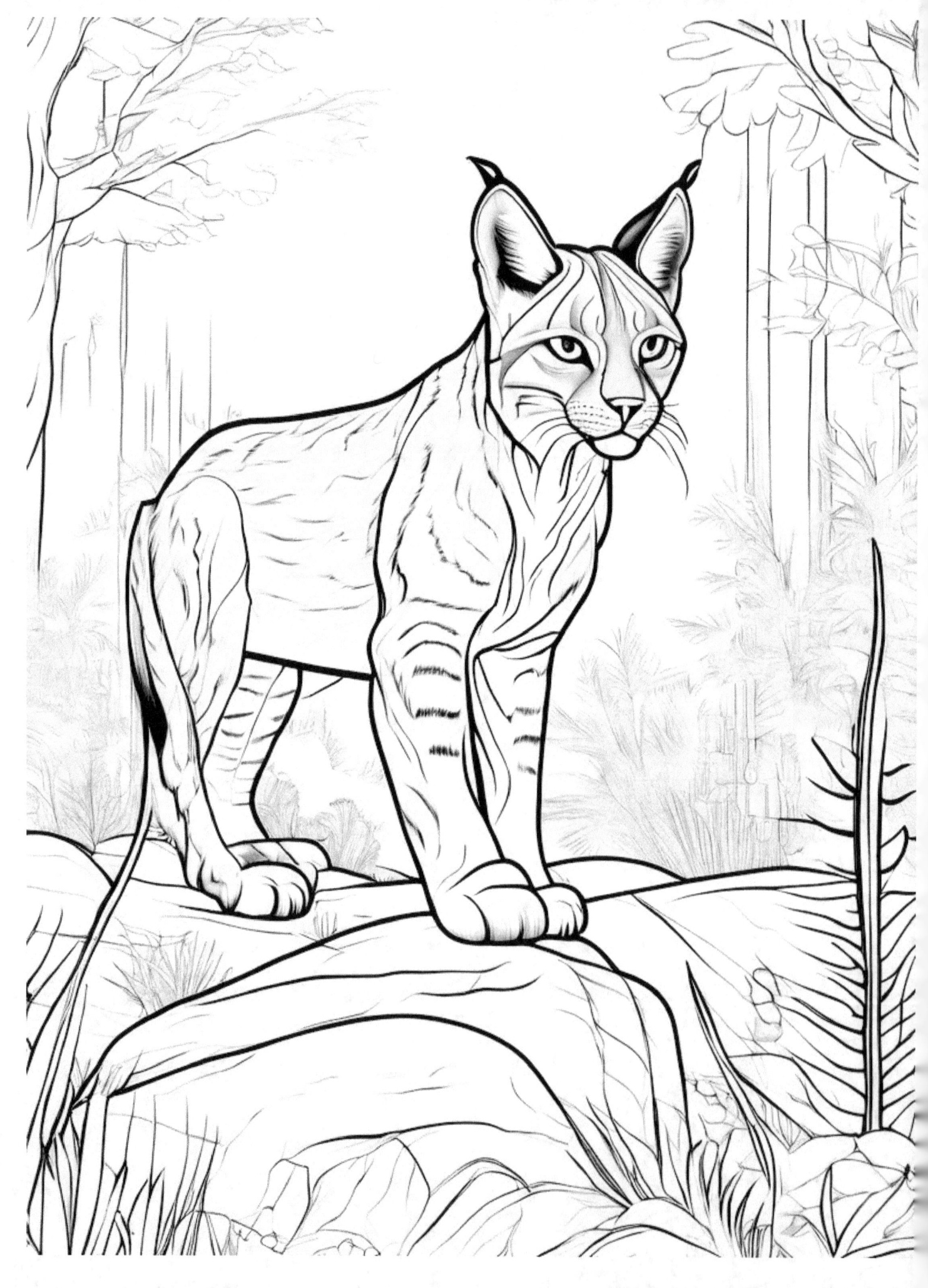

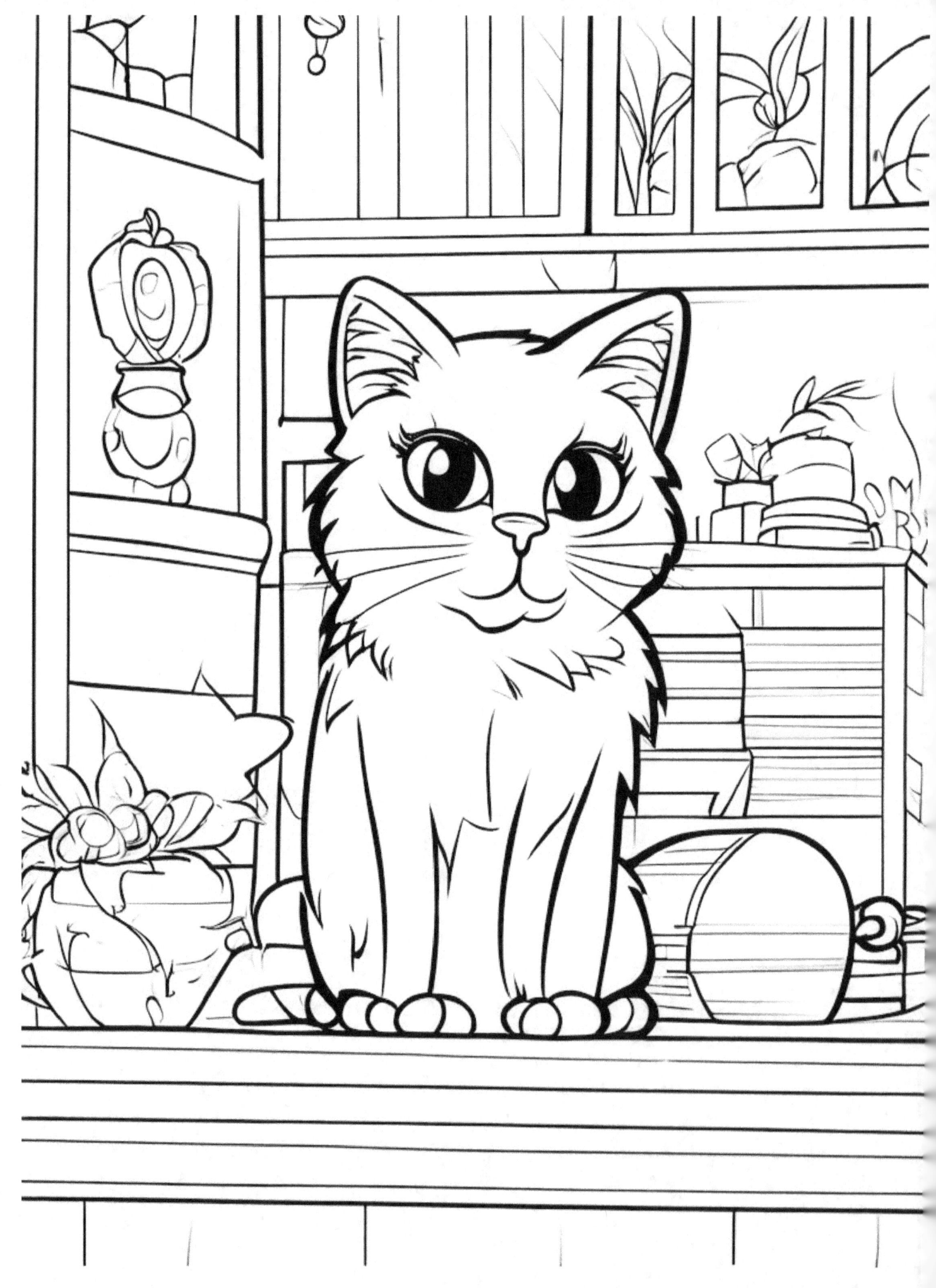

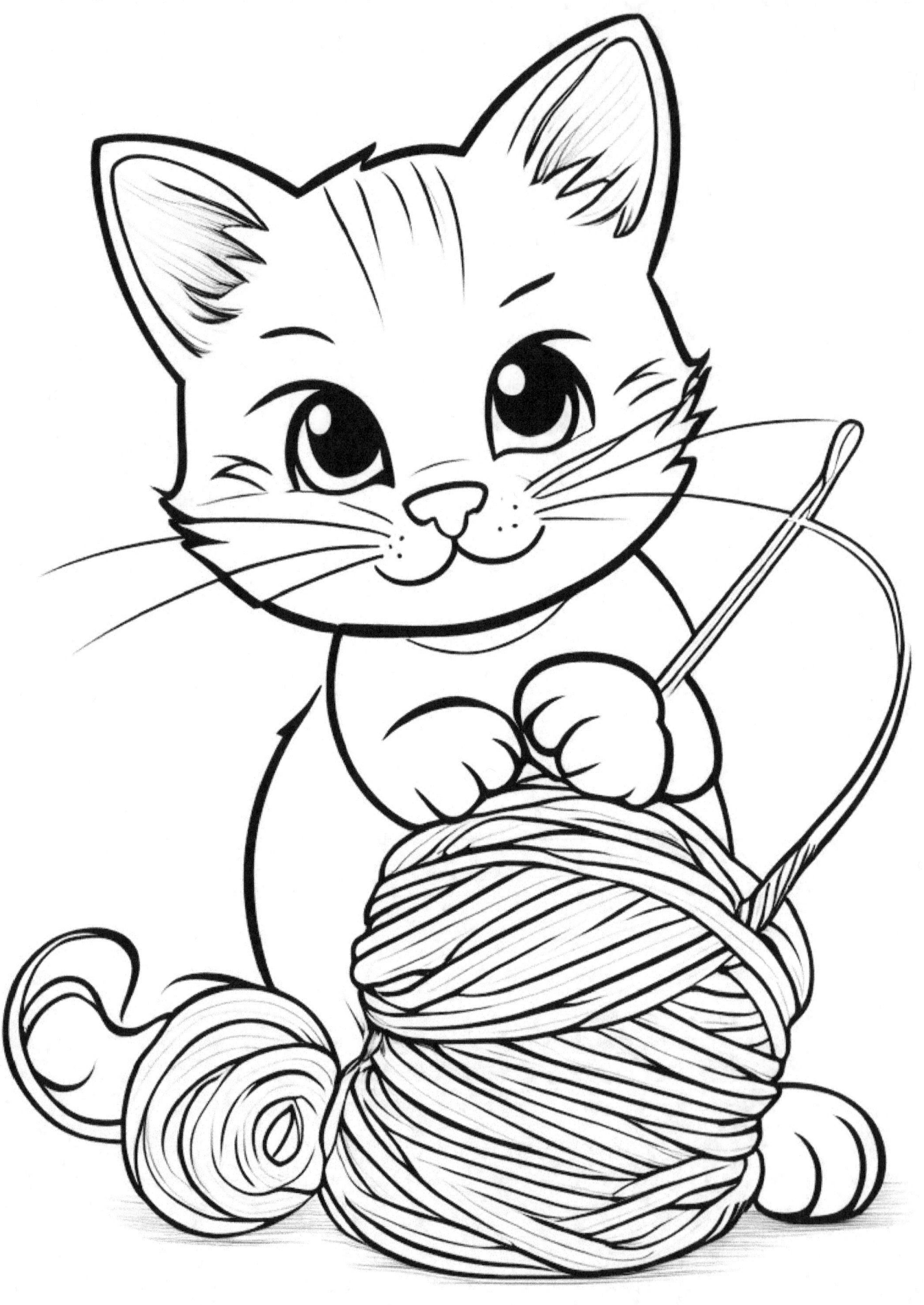

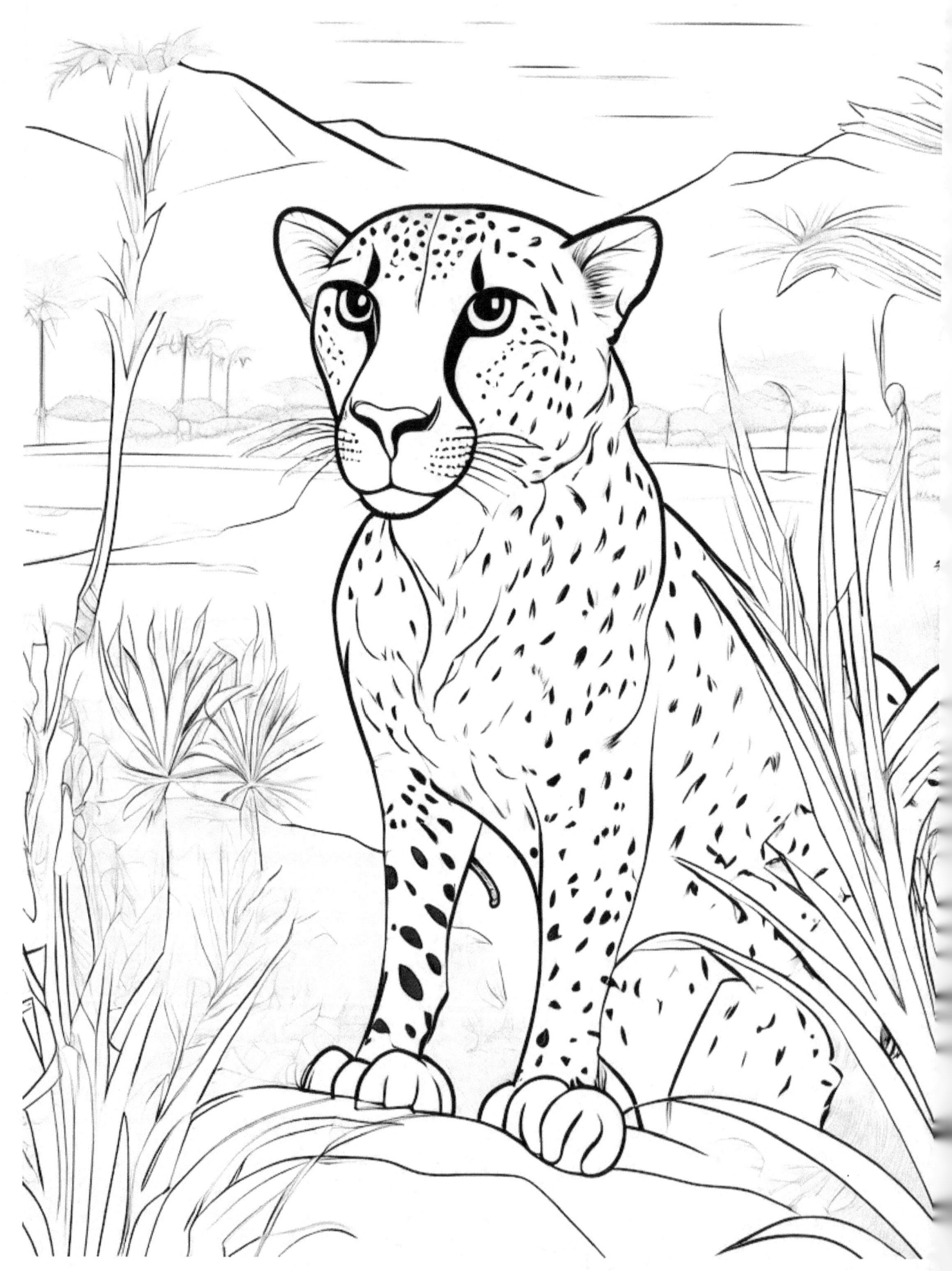

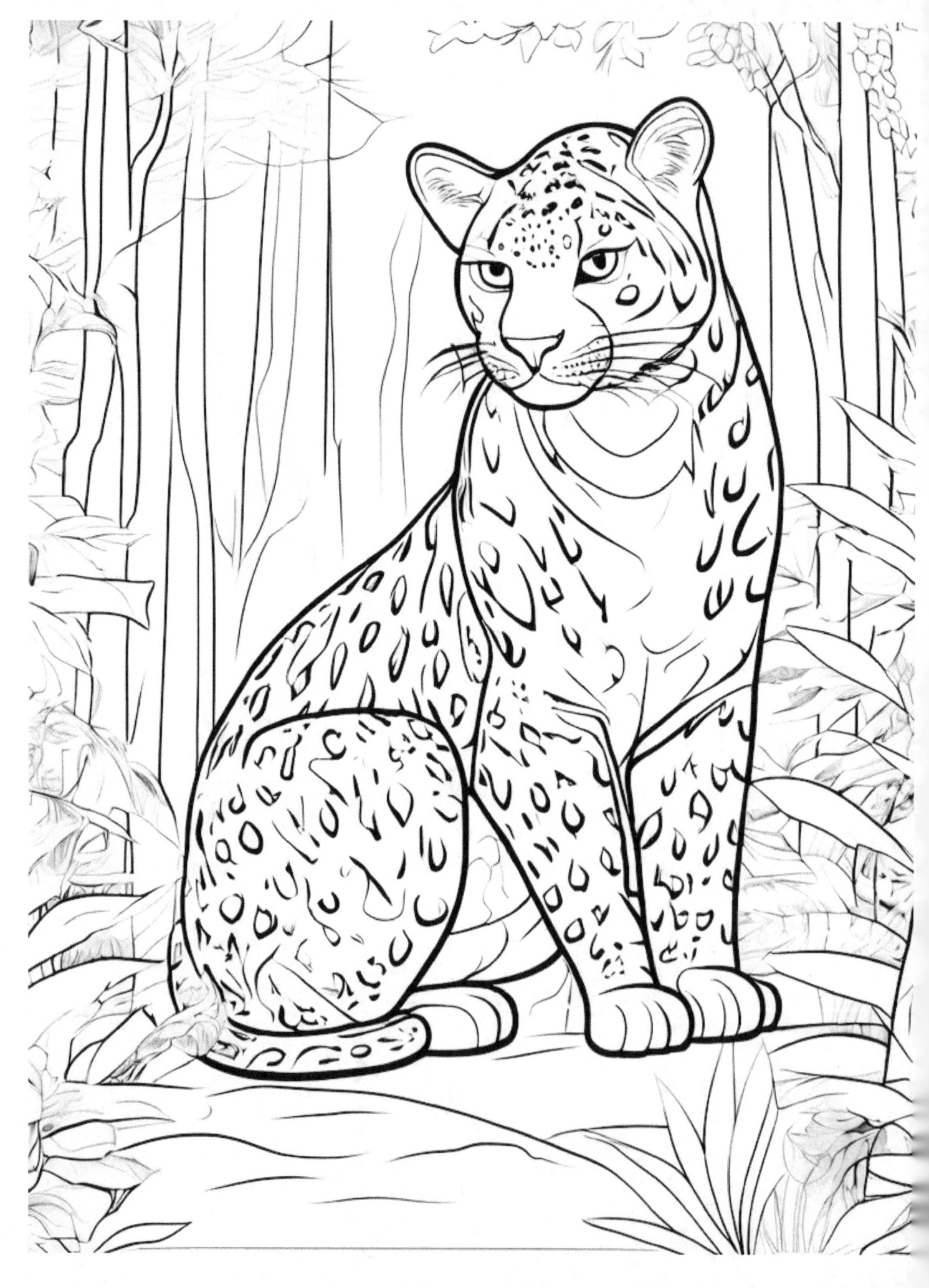

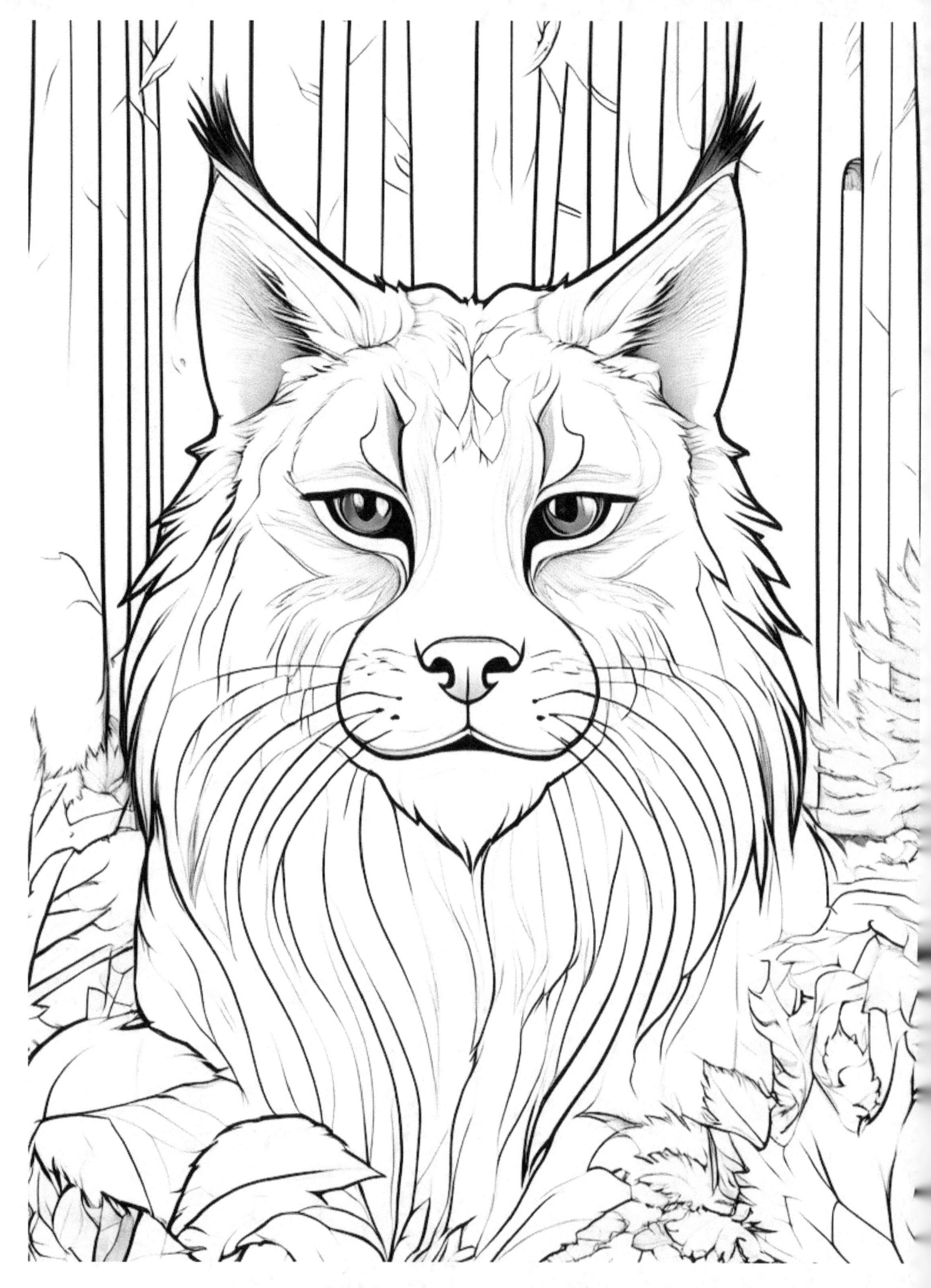

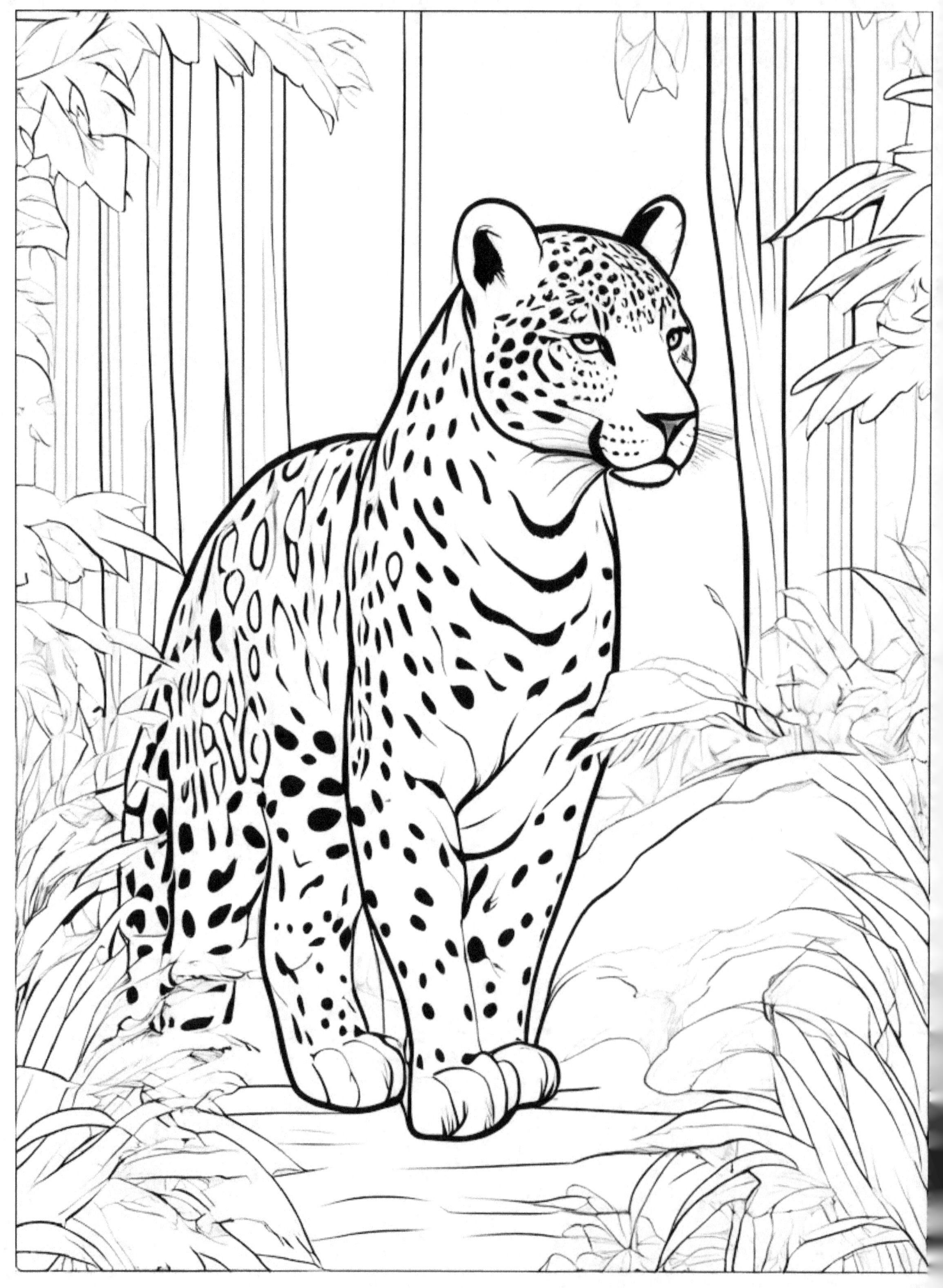

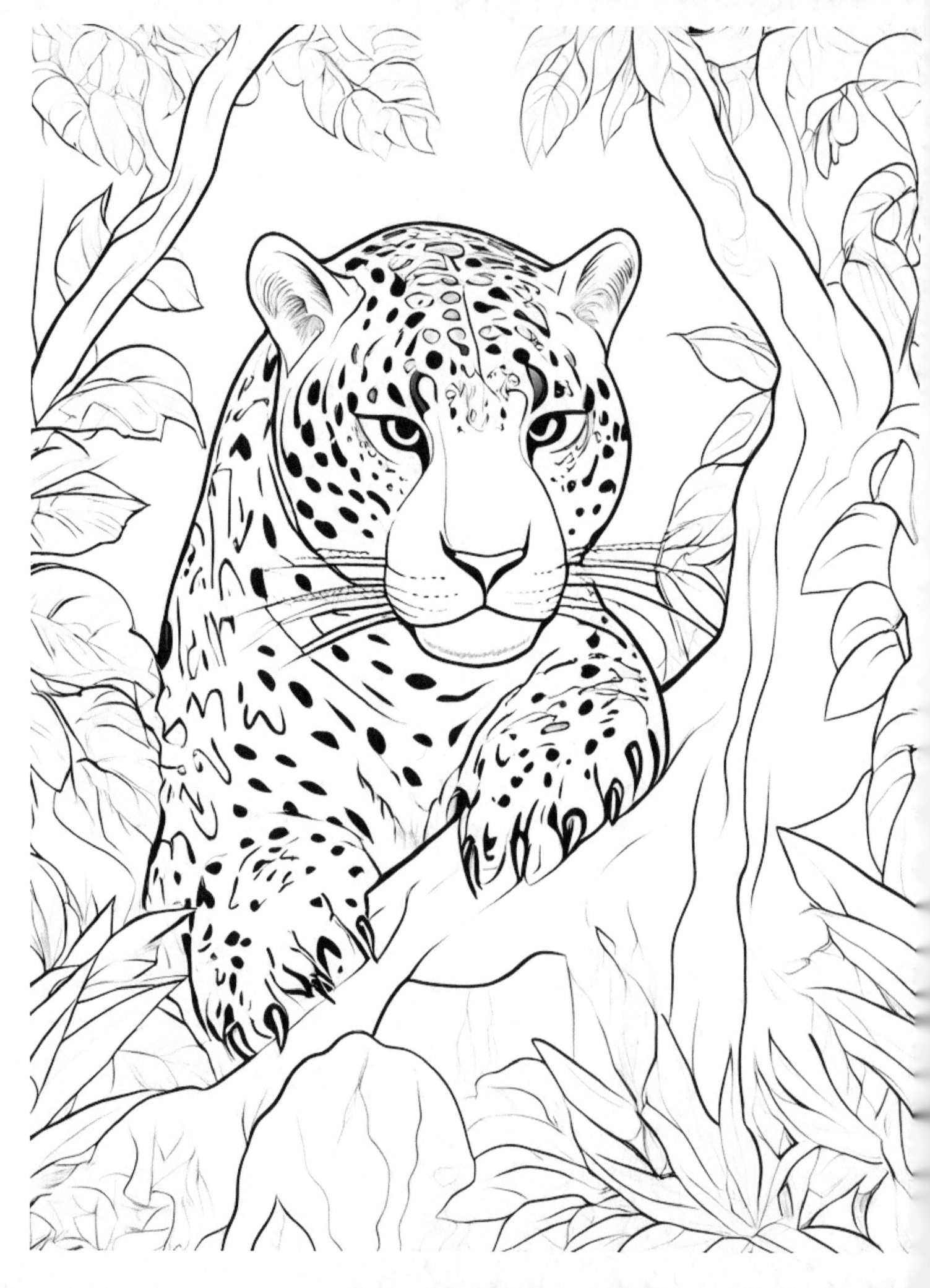

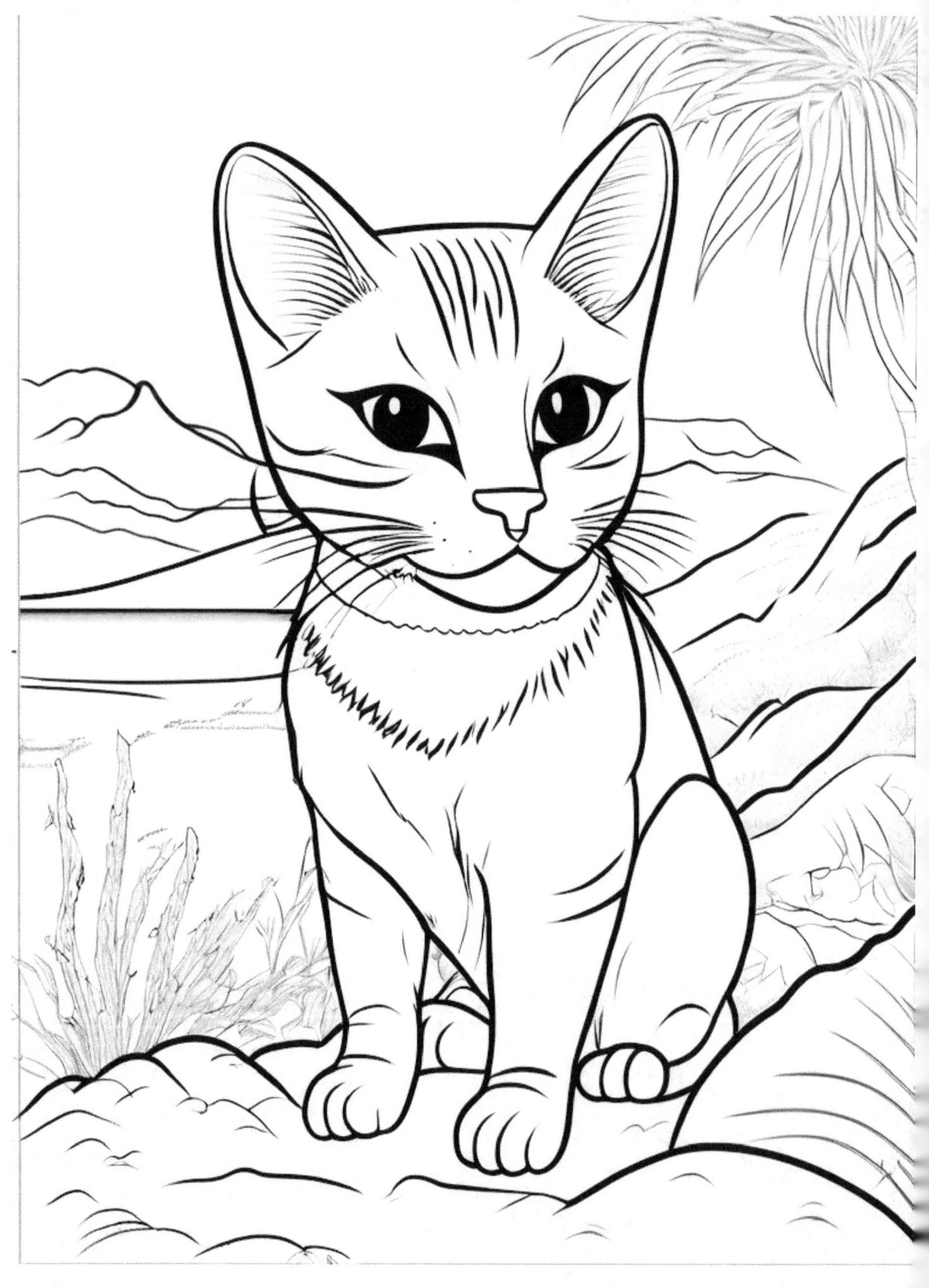

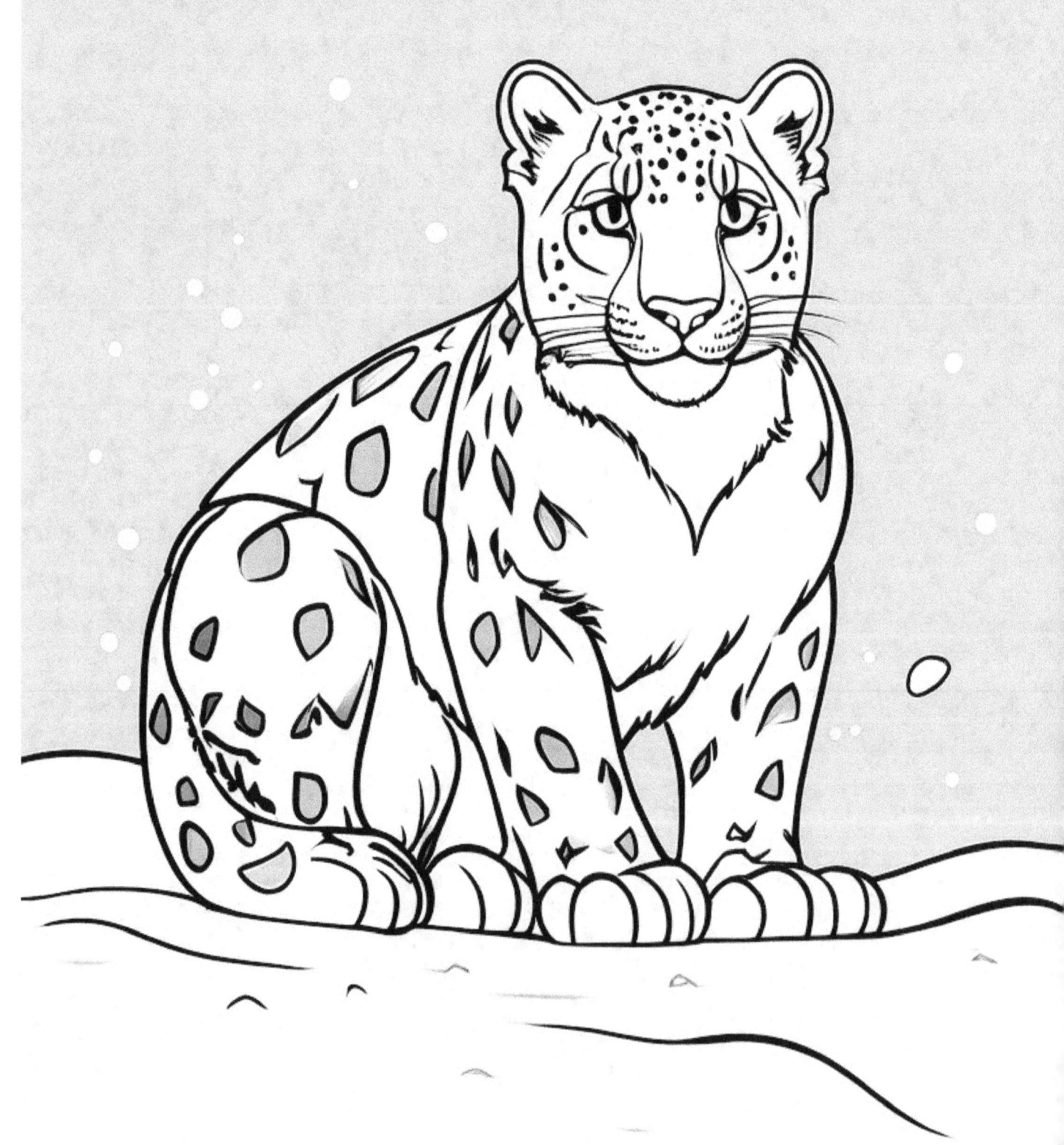

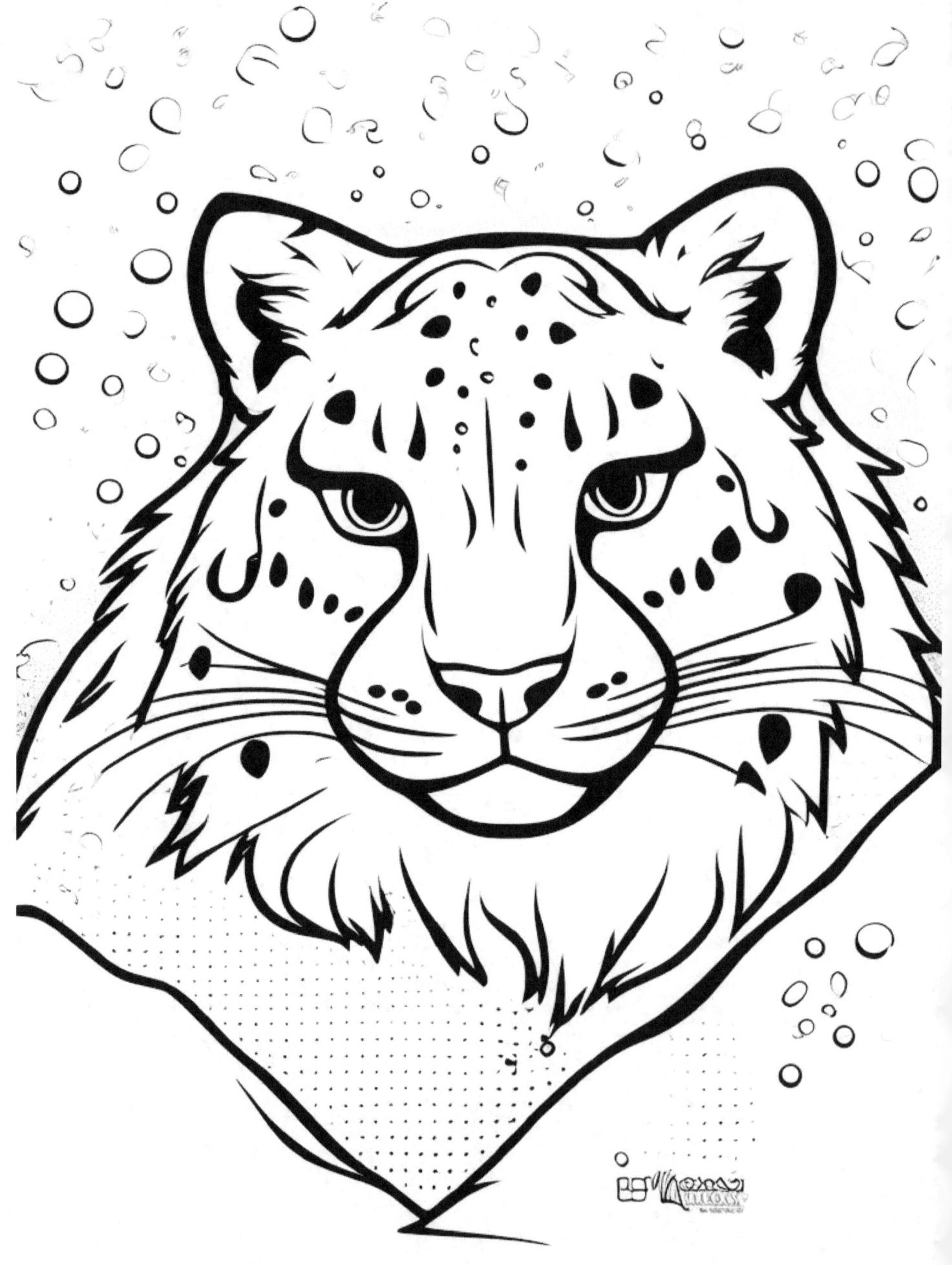

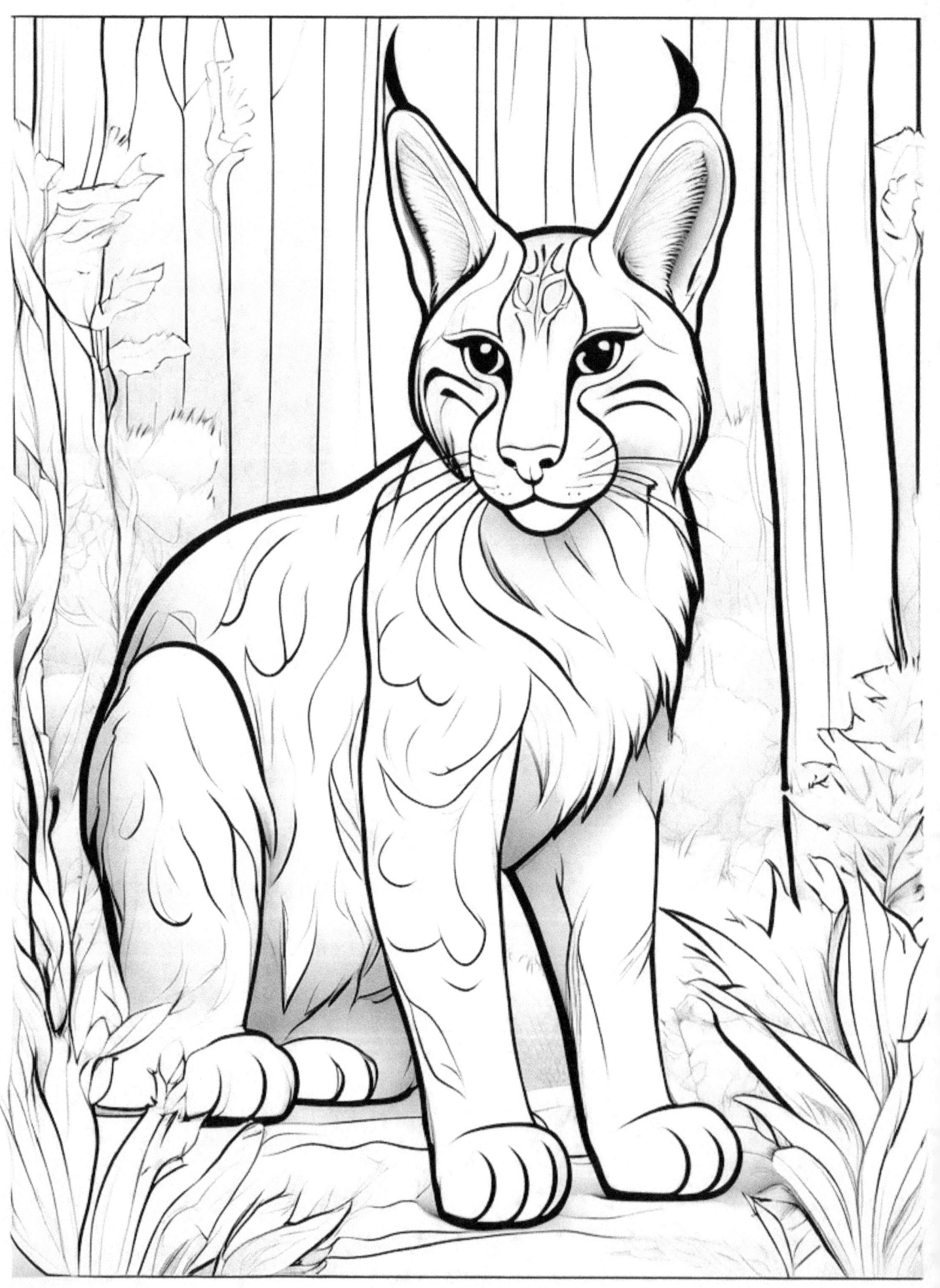

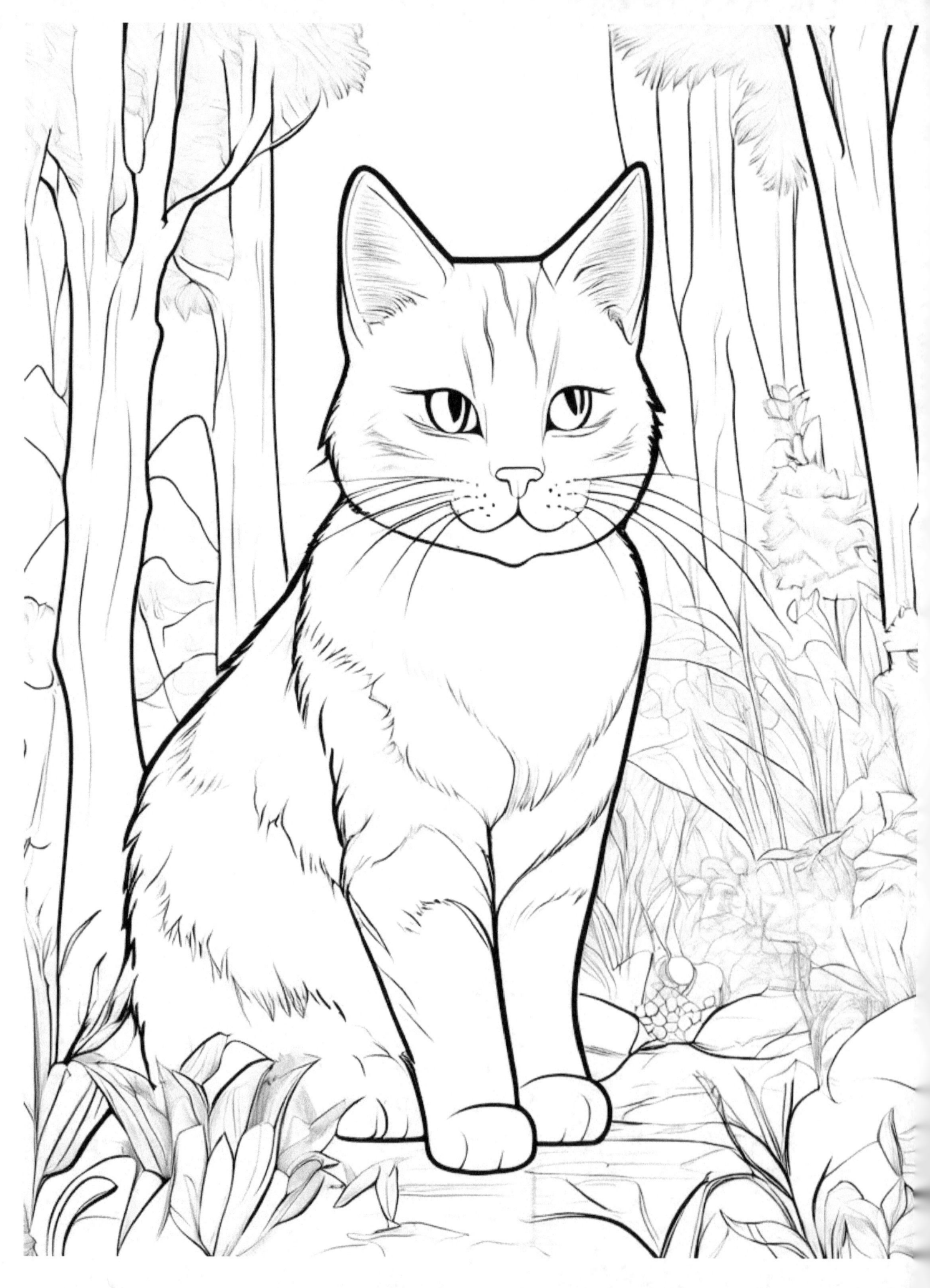

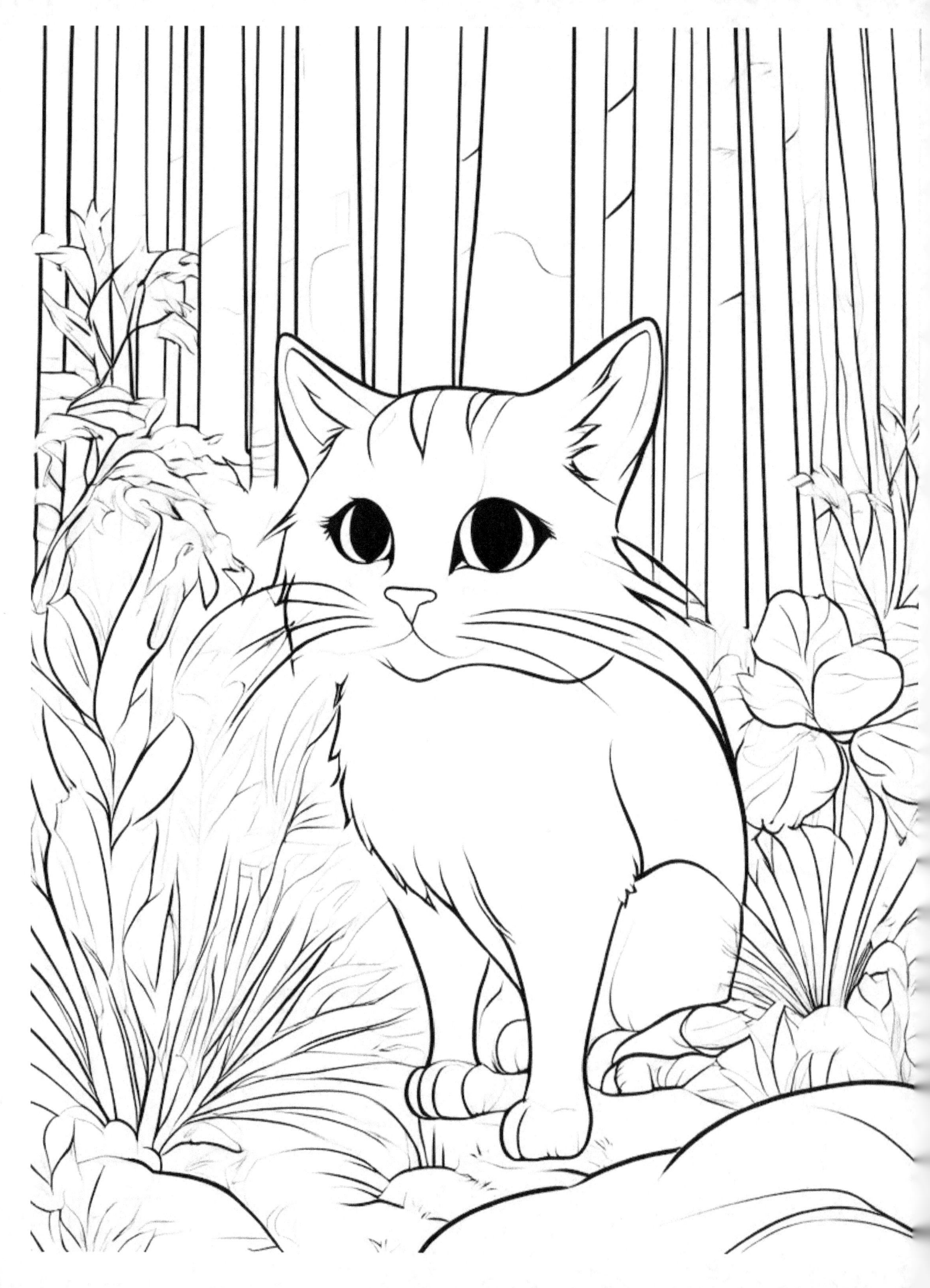

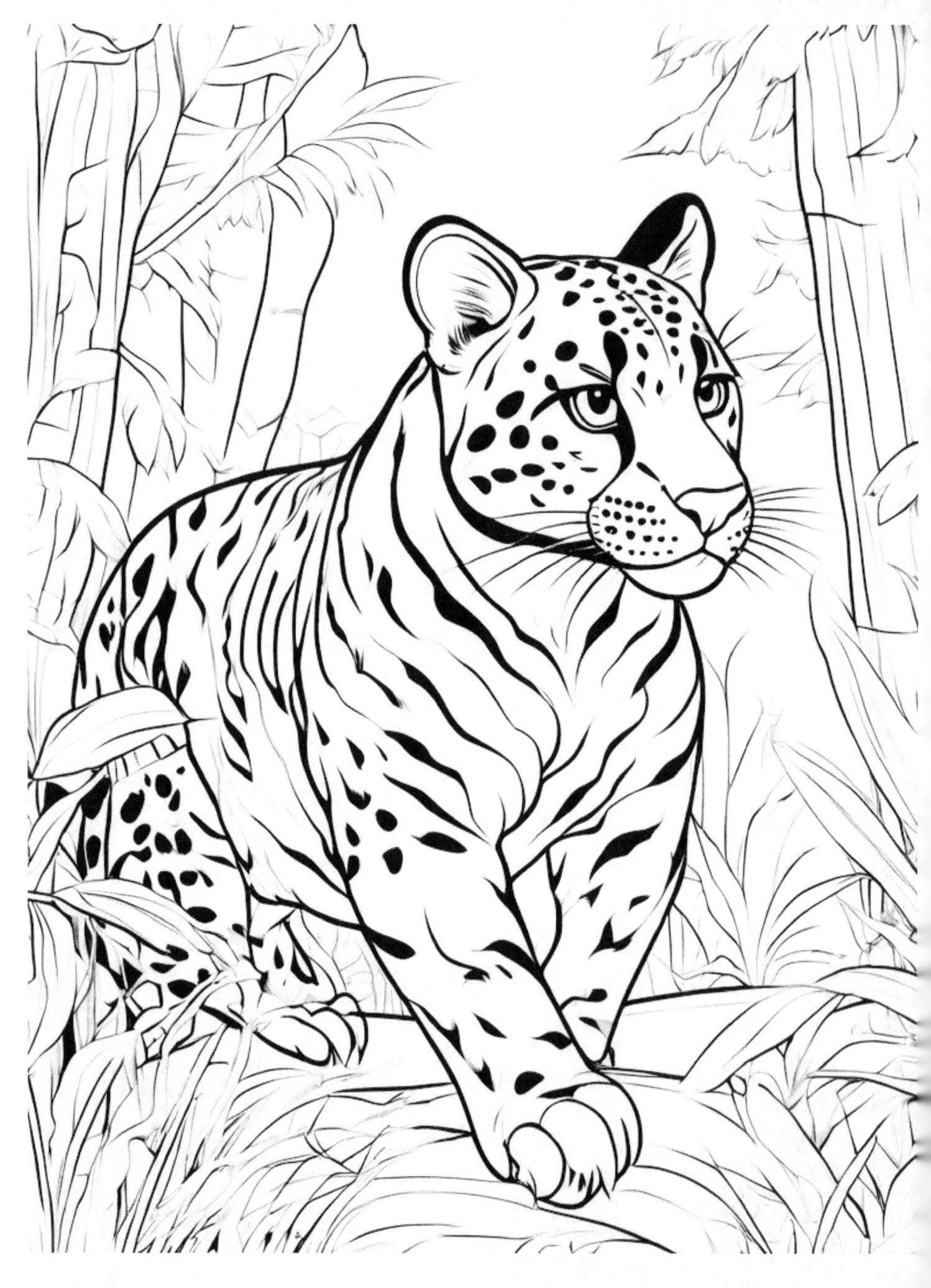

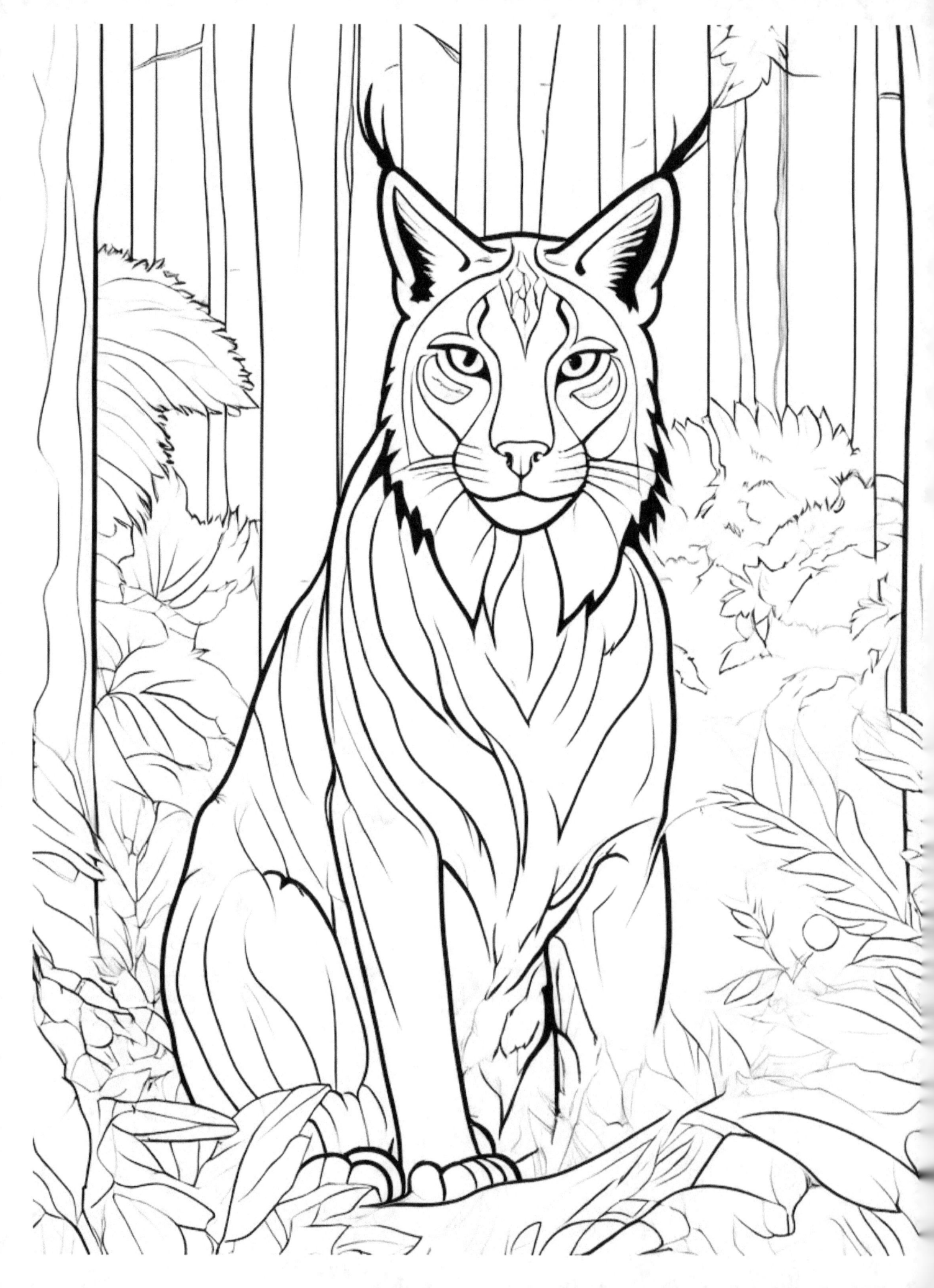

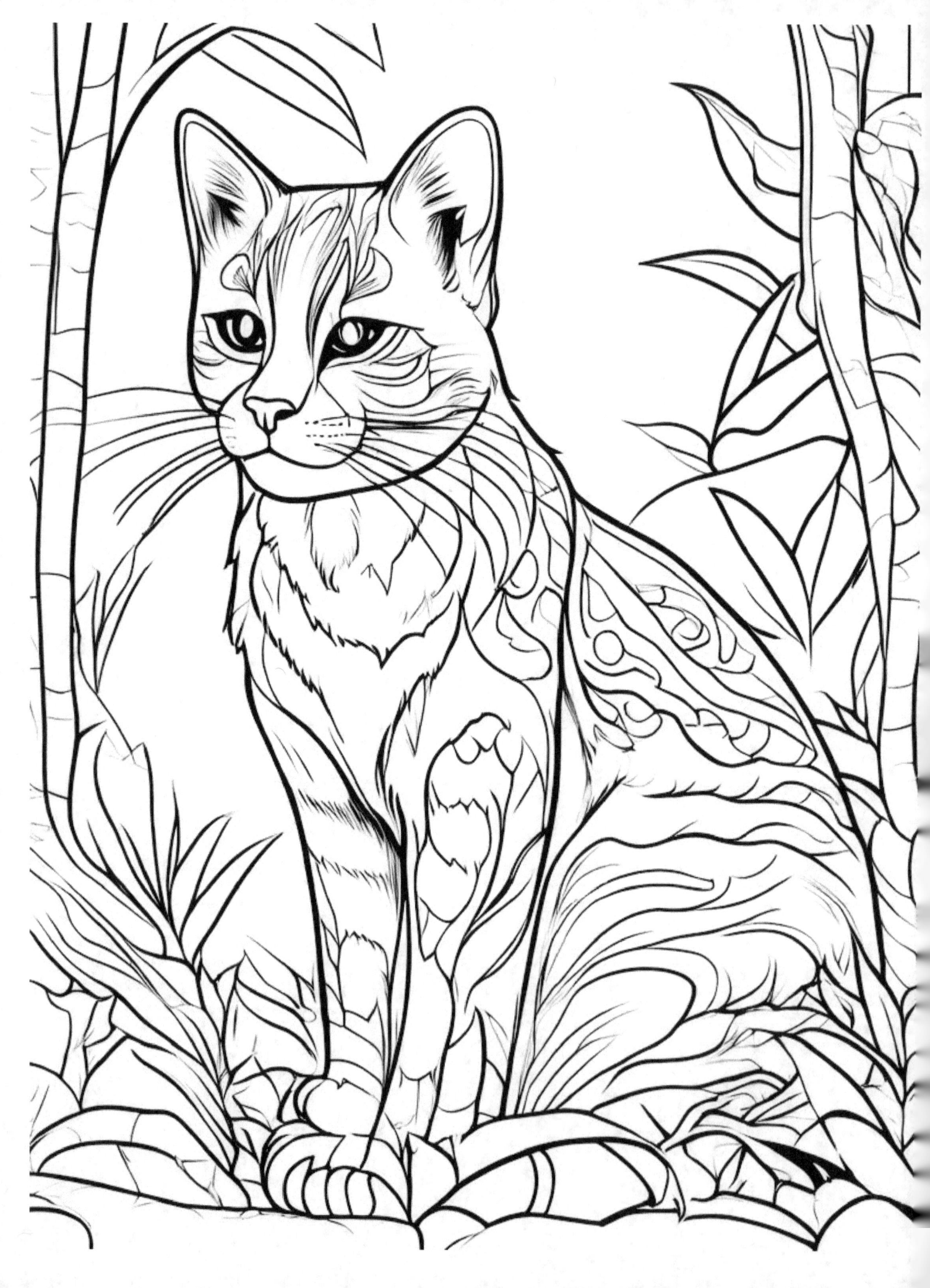

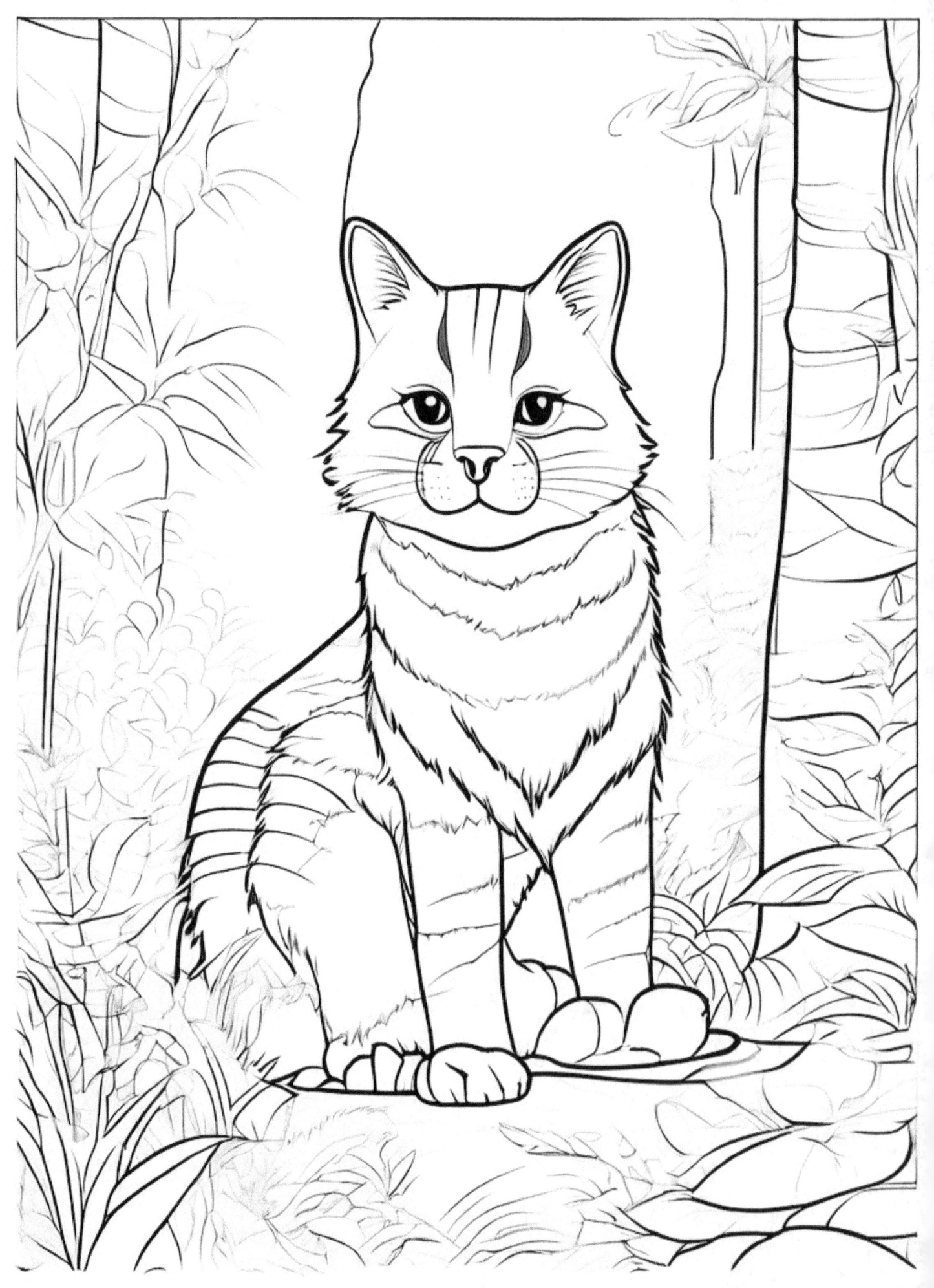

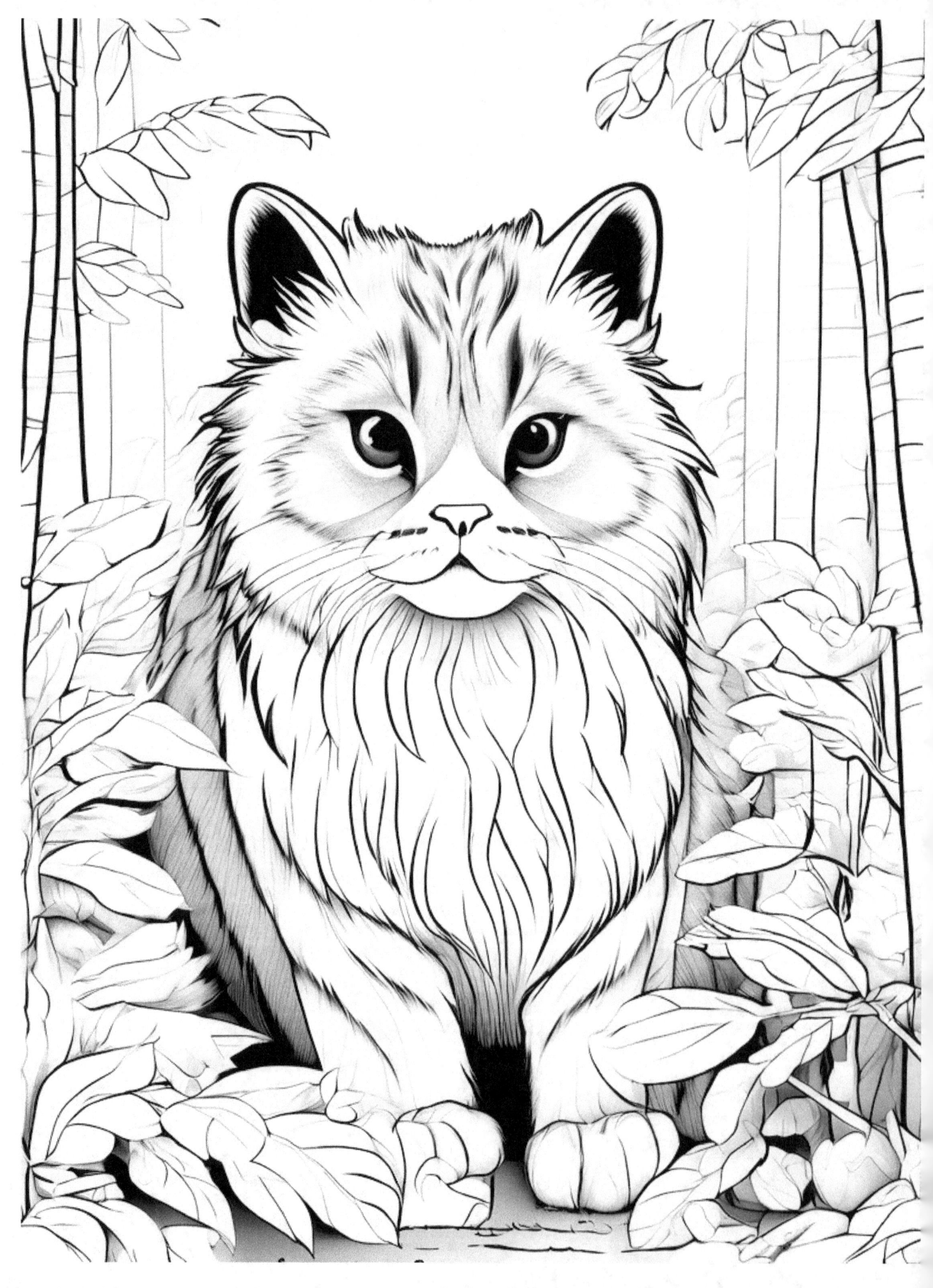

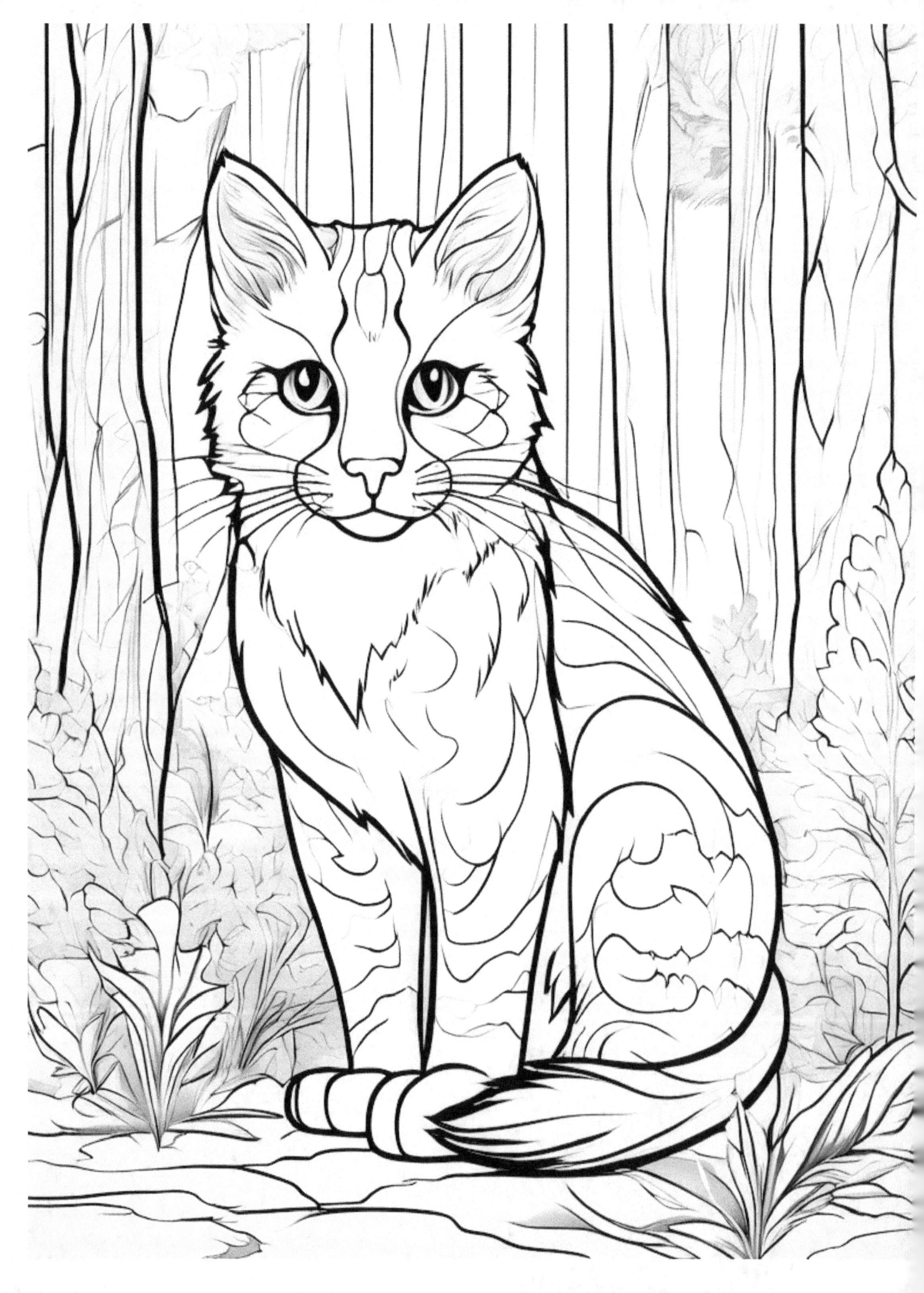

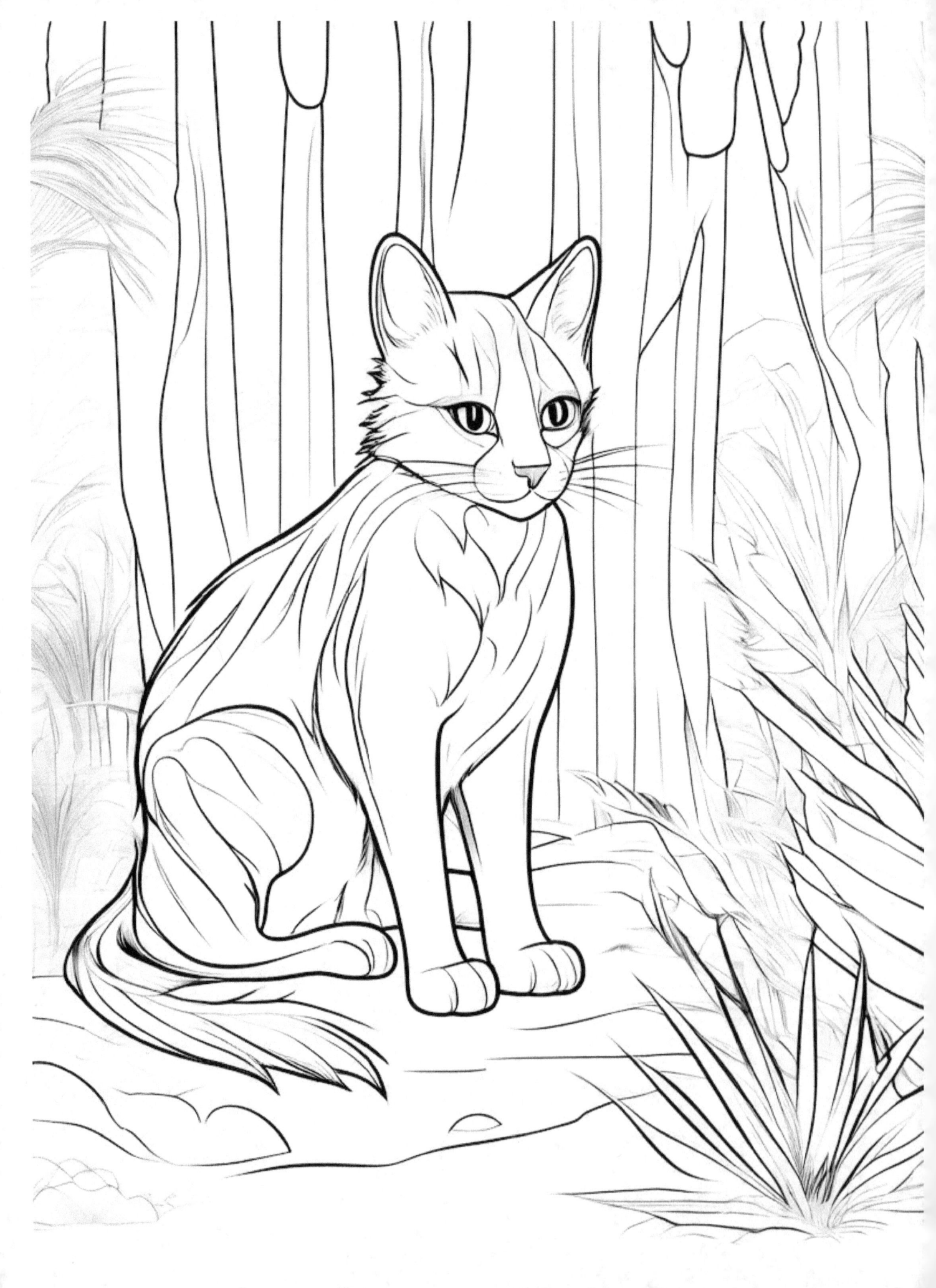

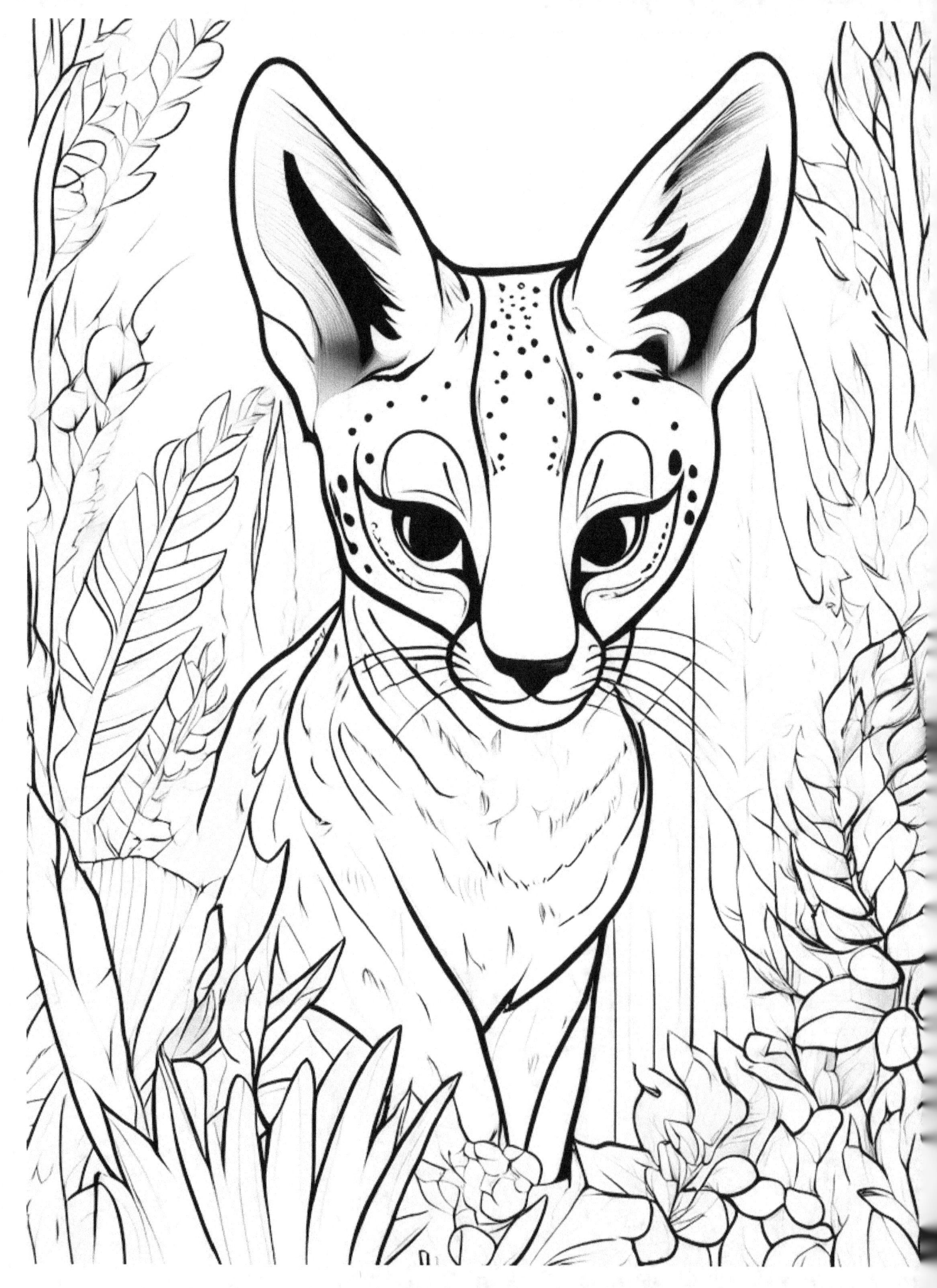

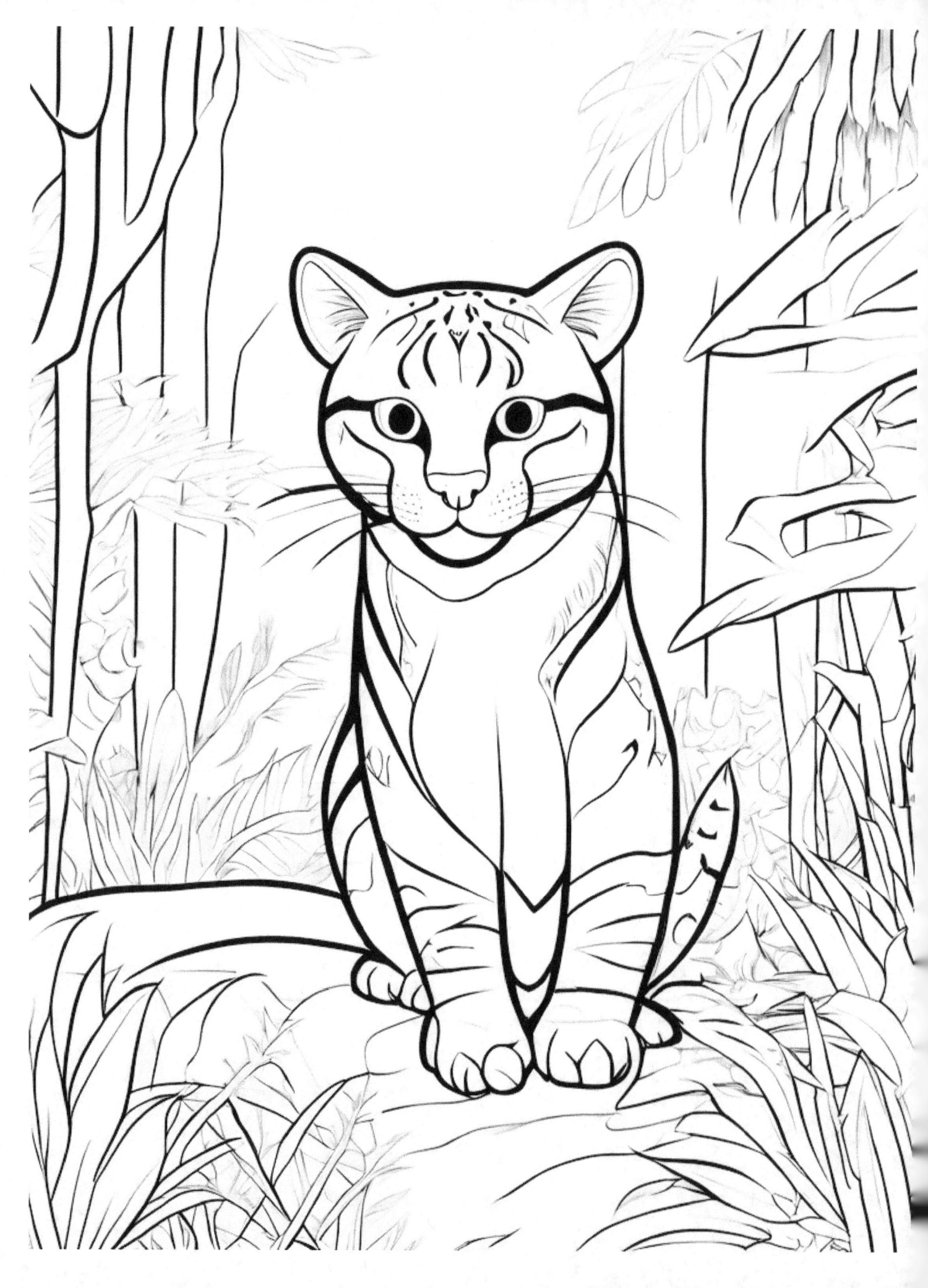

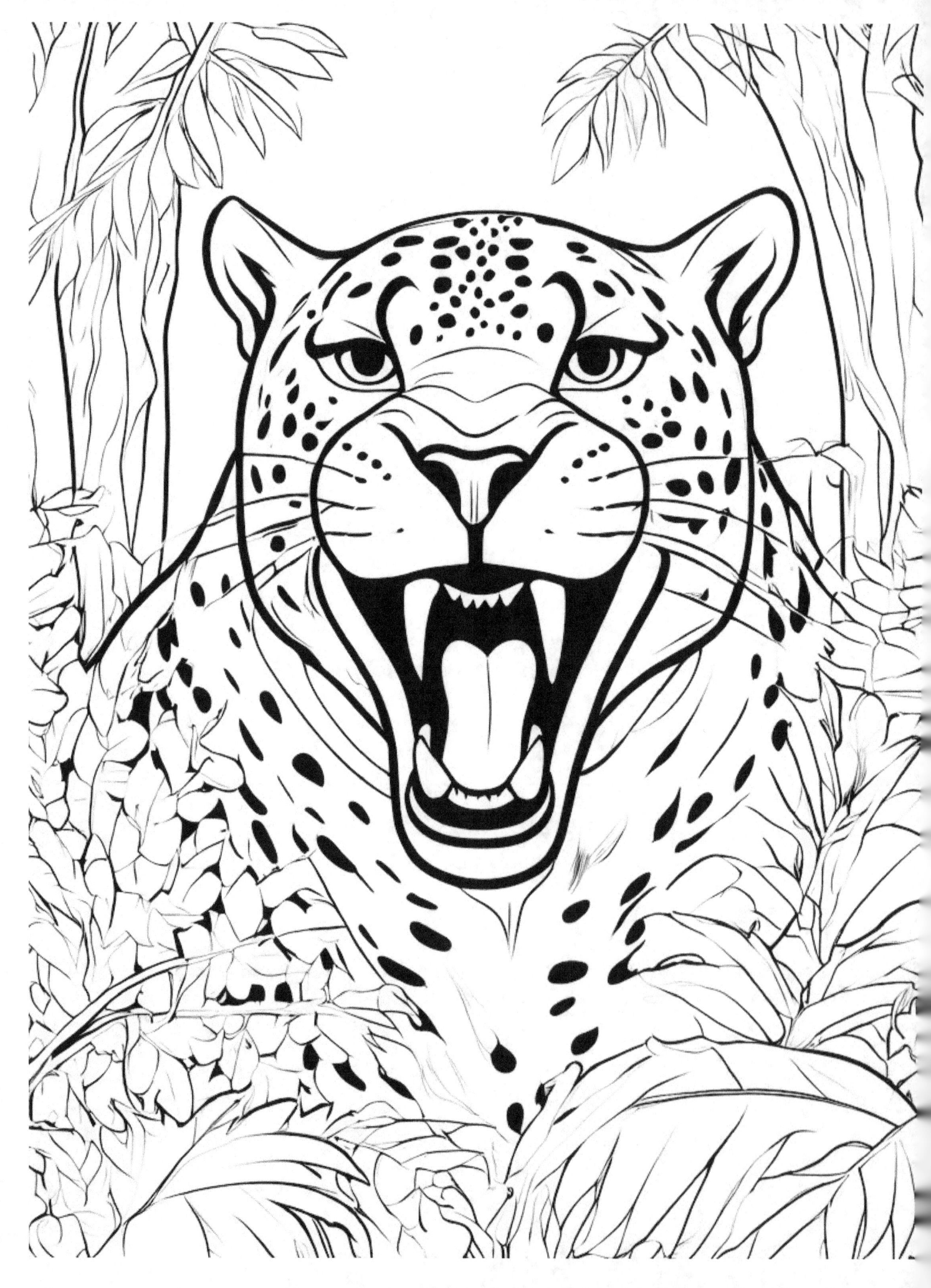

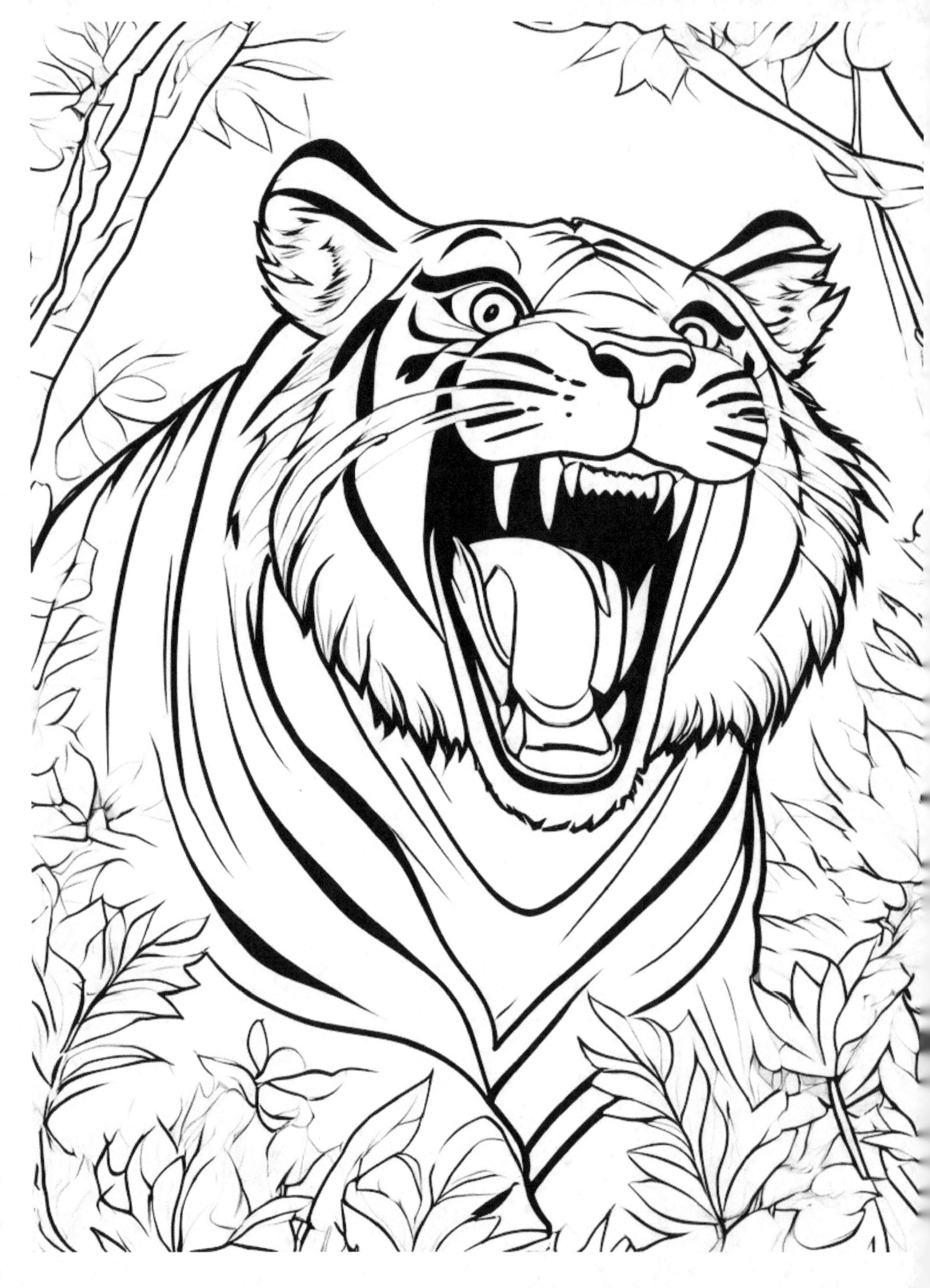

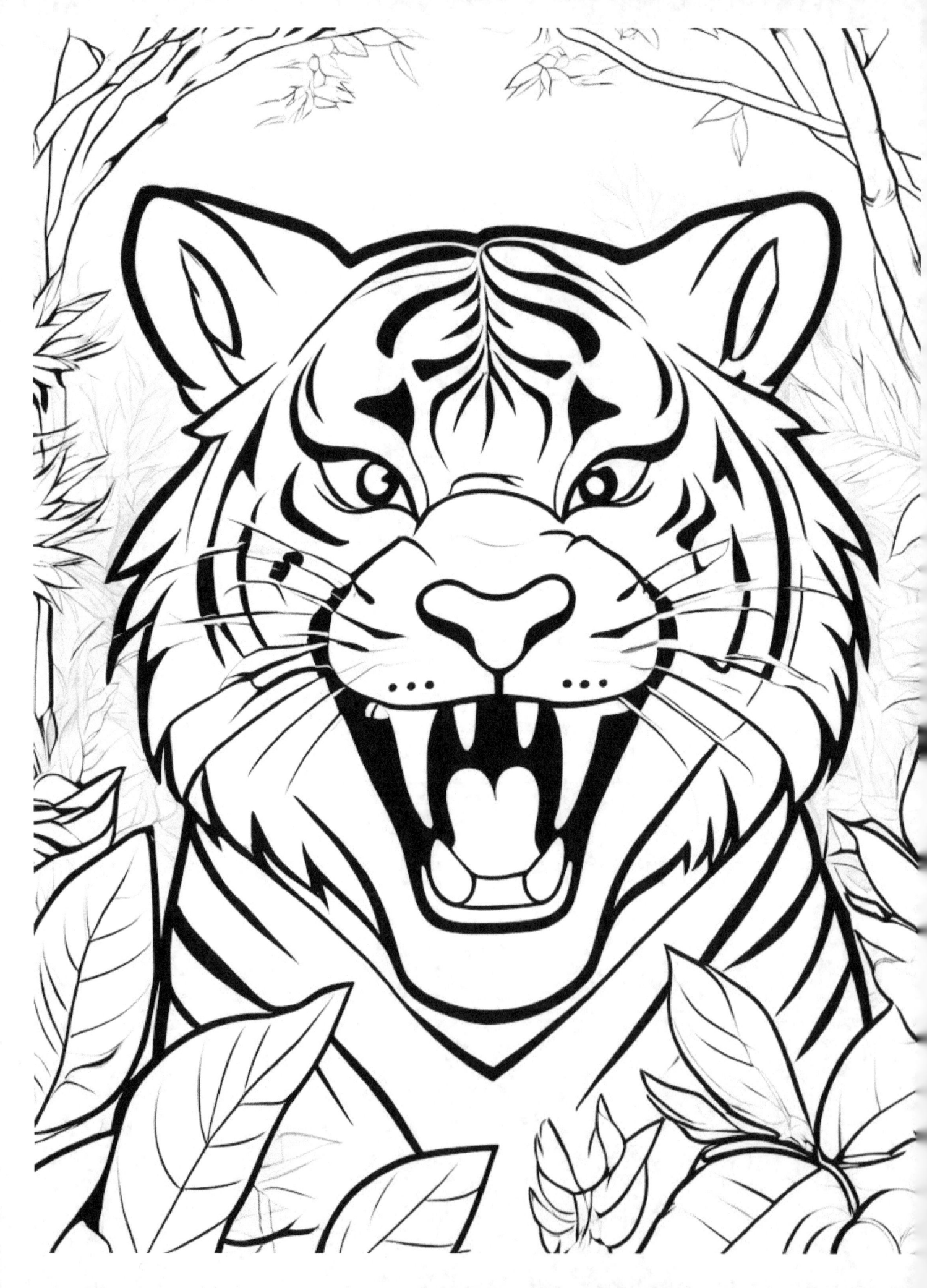

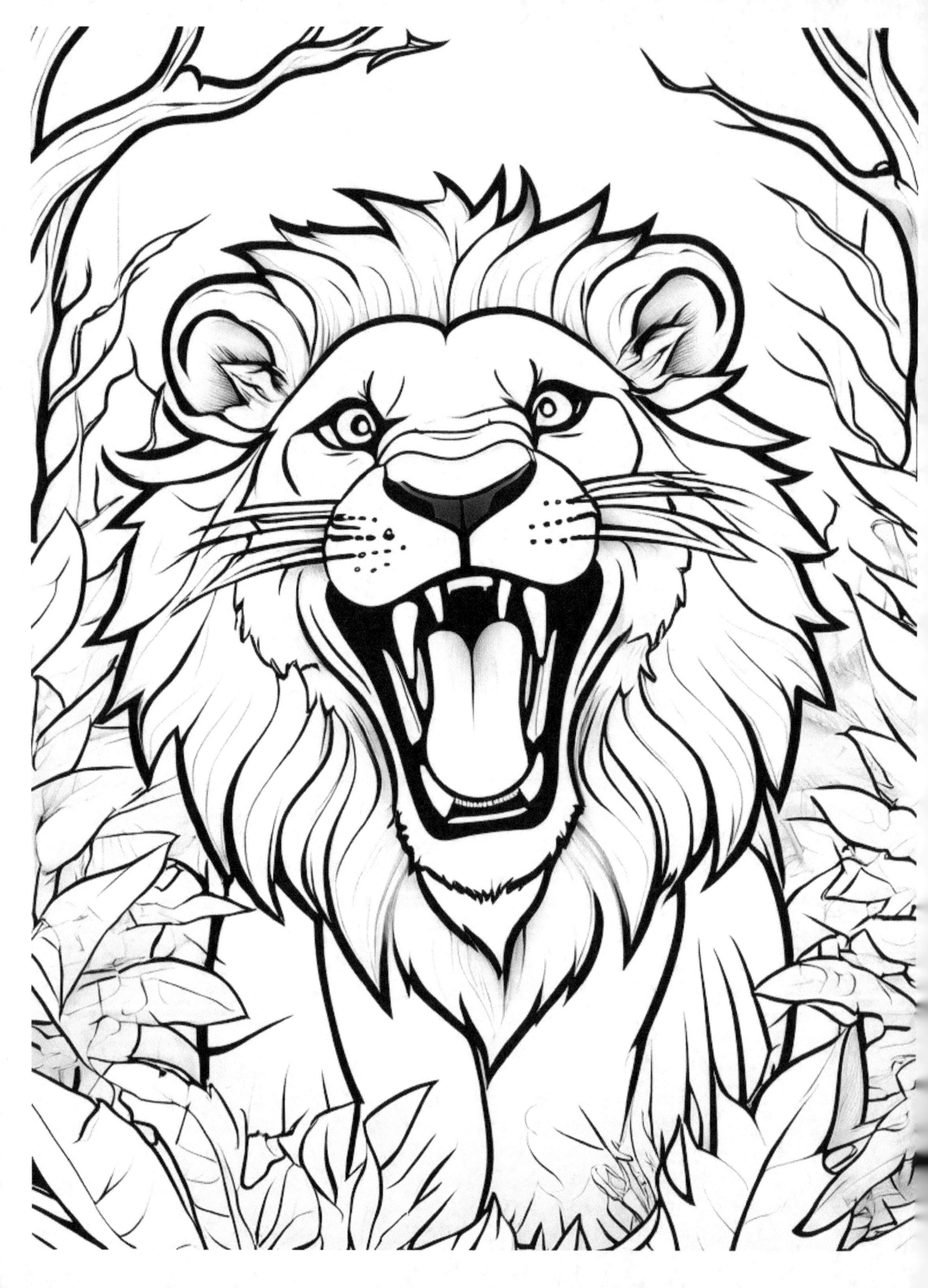

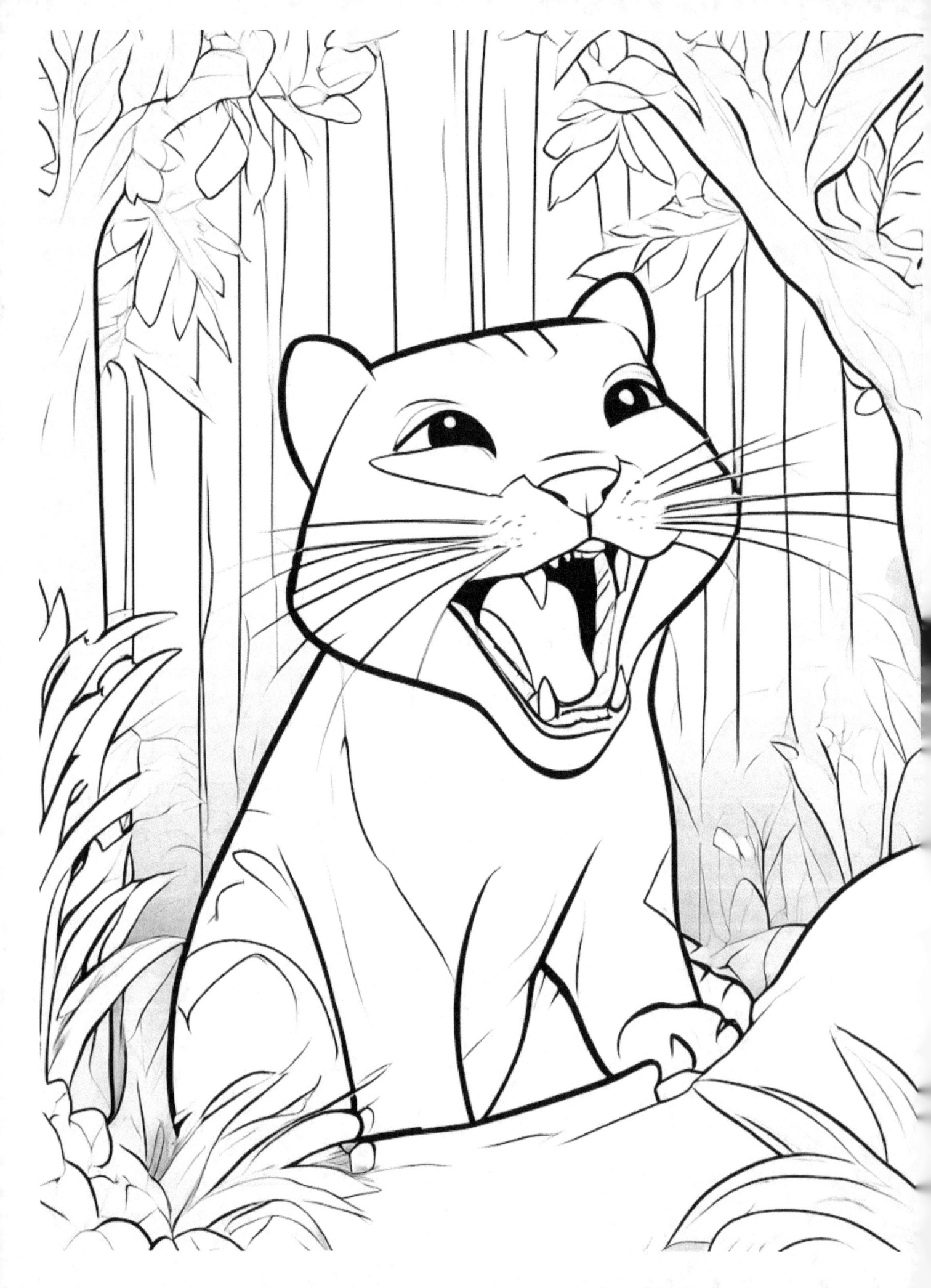

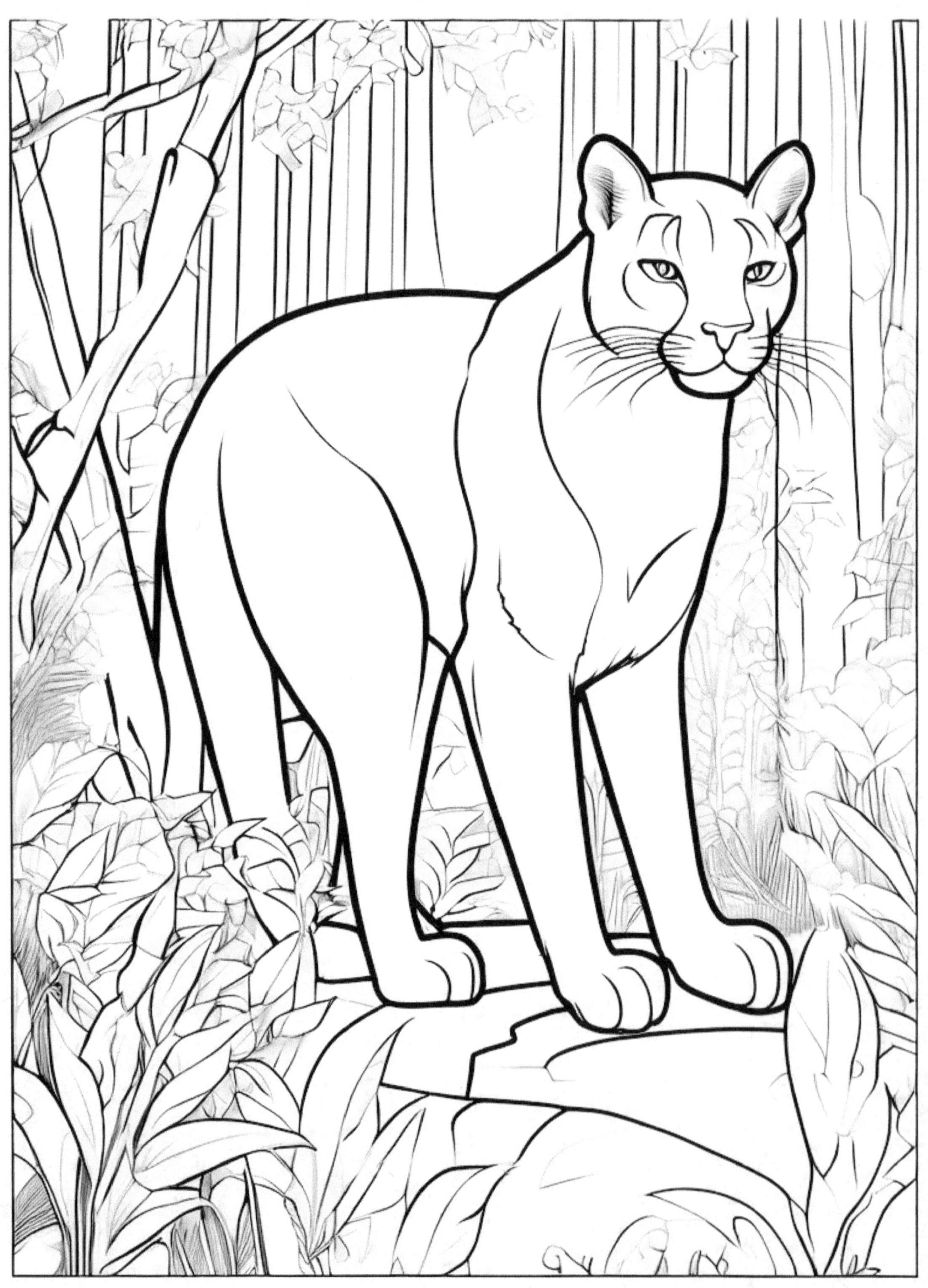

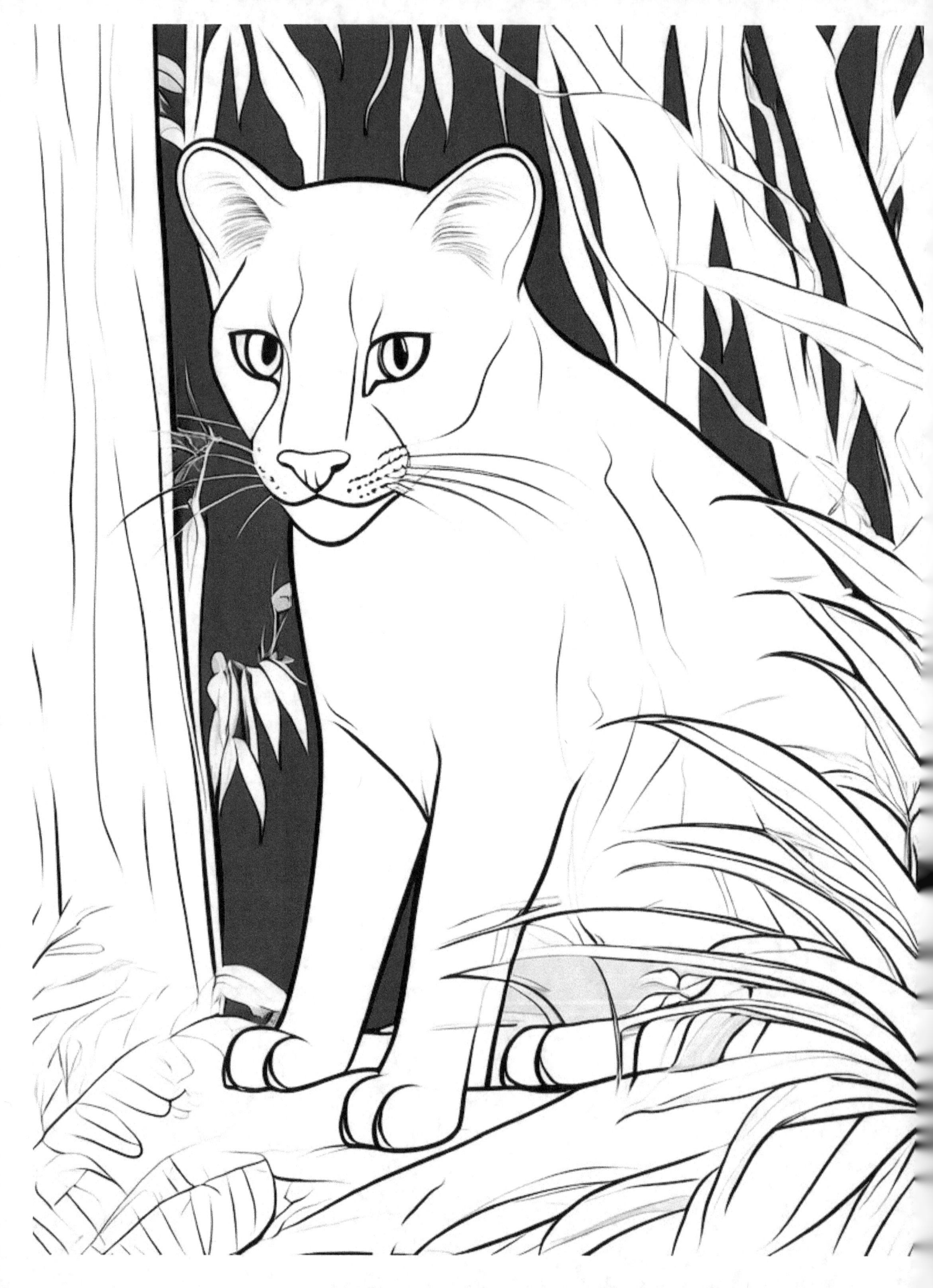

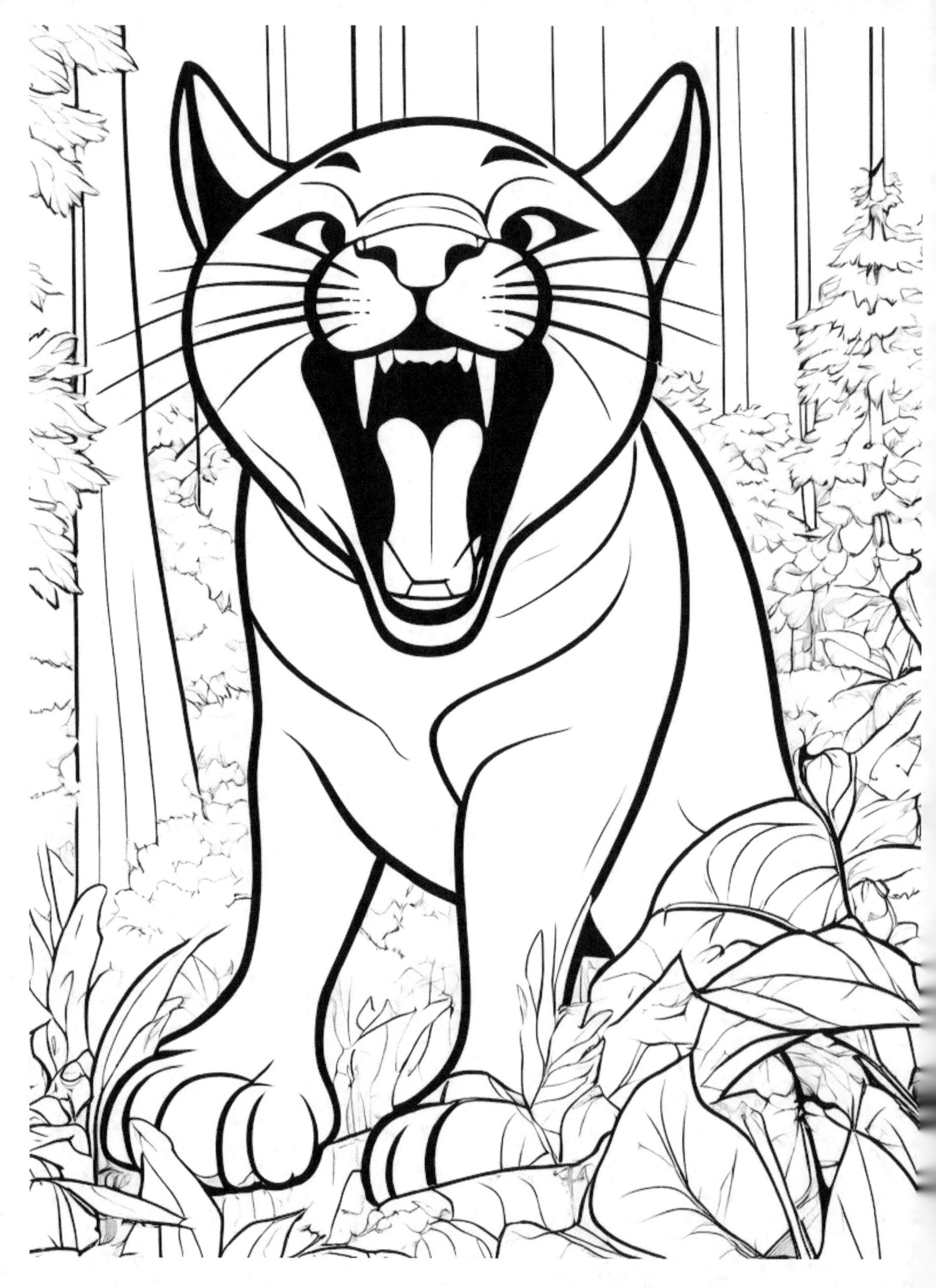

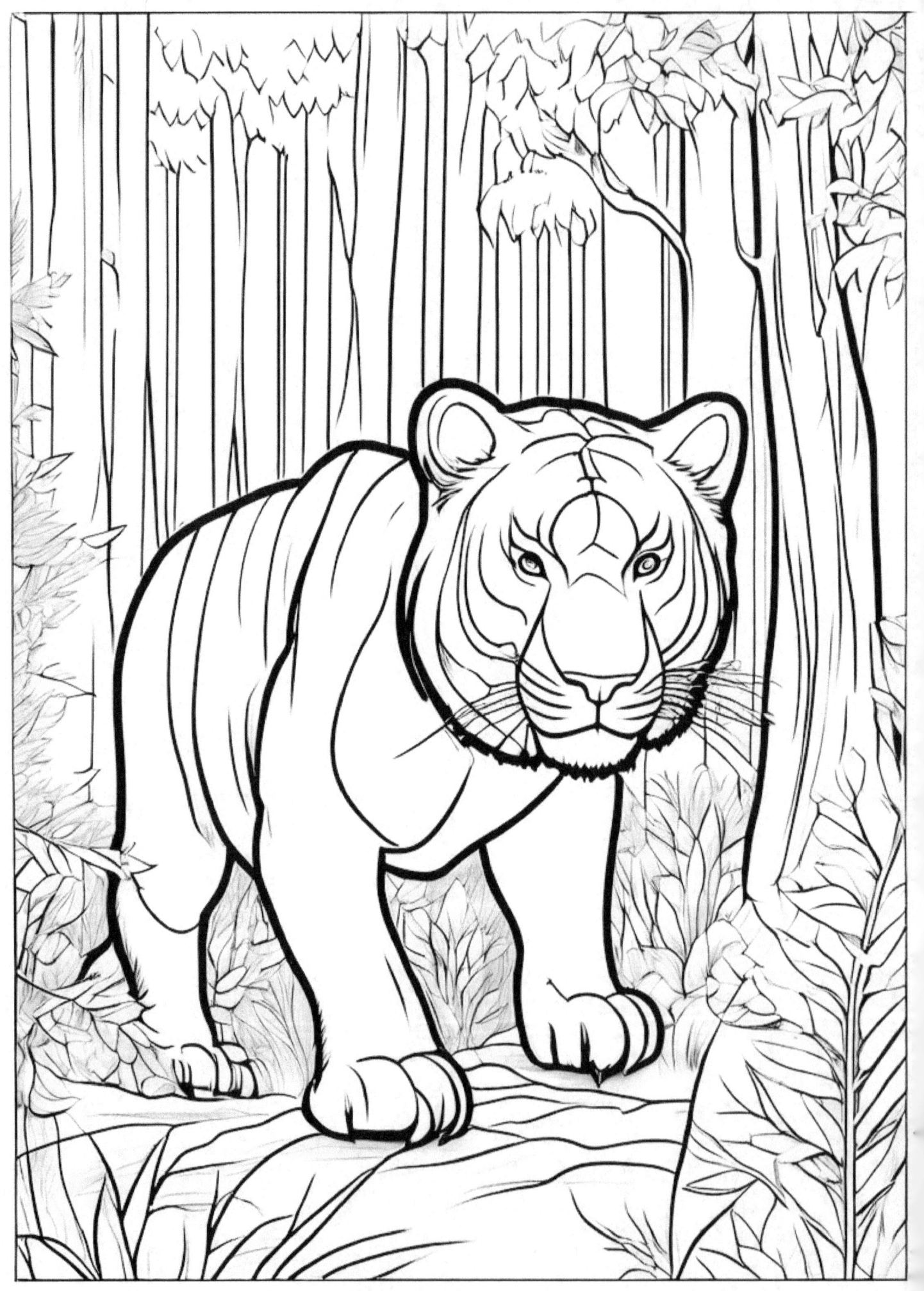

www.ingramcontent.com/pod-product-compliance
Lightning Source LLC
Chambersburg PA
CBHW082215220526
45470CB00010B/3183